W9-AUY-060

On the Wings of Angels

My Years at Saint Mary's Health Care
and the People Who Helped Us Succeed

Philip H. McCorkle, Jr.

as told to Mike Grass

Arbutus Press ✦ Traverse City

On the Wings of Angels: My Years at Saint Mary's Health Care and the People Who Helped Us Succeed, ISBN 978-1-933926-50-6

Library of Congress Cataloging-in-Publication Data
McCorkle, Philip H., Jr.
On the wings of angels : my years at Saint Mary's Health Care and the people who helped us succeed / Philip H. McCorkle, Jr. as told to Mike Grass.
    pages cm
Includes bibliographical references.
 ISBN 978-1-933926-50-6
1. Public health personnel--United States--Biography. 2. McCorkle, Philip H., Jr.--Friends and associates--Biography. 3. Christian biography--Michigan--Grand Rapids. 4. Saint Mary's Health Care (Grand Rapids, Mich.)--History. I. Grass, Michael William. II. Title.
 R153.M38 2013
 362.11092'277456--dc23
 [B]
                              2012042222

BOOK DESIGN BY SUSAN BAYS
PHOTOGRAPHY BY HOYT CARRIER

ARBUTUS PRESS
TRAVERSE CITY, MICHIGAN
EDITOR@ARBUTUSPRESS.COM
WWW.ARBUTUSPRESS.COM

PRINTED IN THE UNITED STATES OF AMERICA

Contents

*Dedicated to all the angels in my life
and to the greatest of angels, my wife, Gayle*

Acknowledgments

"O Lord, who lends me life, lend me a heart
replete with thankfulness."

-William Shakespeare

Claudia Gould, Director of the Institute of Contemporary Art at the University of Pennsylvania in Philadelphia, once said about acknowledgment that, "If I had a single flower for every time I think about you, I could walk forever in my garden." So allow me to take a stroll through my figurative backyard plot and thank the people who helped in the creation of this book. Yes, I could walk for hours, perhaps forever, and encounter angels at every turn and bloom! Next to those I may not mention, through oversight and omission, there are countless people who contributed invaluable information and counsel for this book. Their help is gratefully acknowledged.

It comes as no surprise that Grand Rapids is an intimate and special community, especially among its Catholic congregants. Everyone seems to know someone who knows someone. That is how our community works. We are all connected by the ties of love that bind us together. The people featured in this book know that far better than I. But without these candid glimpses into their novel lives, their lives as angels among us, where their individual stories are not often known or shared, at least to this degree, there would be no book. And so with their imprint on these pages, they will forever remain my angels and my friends, and close friends of

Saint Mary's Health Care. And so in no particular order, I wish to thank the following people:

I am indebted to **Father Mark Przybysz**, whose knowledge of our subjects is as far and wide as it is deep. I thank him for casting light on the shining faces throughout our book and their gracious Catholic lives.

I thank **Sister Patrice Konwinski** for sharing her story of the late Bishop Kevin Britt, such a painful chapter for her and for all of us.

I gratefully thank **Mary Haarman**, former Director of Communications for the Diocese of Grand Rapids, for her humor, her openness and her vast knowledge of all things Catholic. Her smile is as infectious as her sparkling eyes are wide. Thank you, Mary!

And without **Monsignor Bill Duncan**, this would be a lesser work indeed. His eloquence and overview cannot be ignored. Without him, *On the Wings of Angels* would be a mere idea without a focus, blank pages without words, effort without expression. So thank you, Bill Duncan. You are as much an angel as a saint!

I thank **Nancy Skinner** who helped me take an idea and turn it into this book. In her own right, she is an angel indeed who nurtured this project through. This all began with her. It was Nancy who first introduced me to my writing partner, **Mike Grass**, the engine behind this work and its creative spark. I thank Mike for his wonderful way with words, his passion for research, his fluency and his literary skill. Where would I be in this venture without him?

While **John Canepa** is featured as one of our angels in this book, he is our altar boy; he served us as a wonderful resource. He knows everyone and everything about our city and its citizens, Catholic and otherwise. Thank you, John, for being a part of our book and for your invaluable help in its research.

I gratefully acknowledge **Micki Benz** for her help and wonderful guidance, insight and counsel. Saint Mary's Health Care would be a lesser place without her; we have worked so well together.

My executive assistant, **Carol Dirkse,** is like my right hand. Wherever I am or go, Carol is there. I thank her for being with us throughout this marvelous journey.

And there are others for sure who played large and small parts, some unknowingly. I thank **John Benz** for his candor and for his fine and long memory about his friend, Bob Herr. I thank **Dr. David Blair** for nurturing and championing Advantage Health and for his knowledge of, and comments about, our doctor healers, like Paul Farr. I thank **Jim Brady** and **John Byington** for helping us remember and revere Ken Hungerford; thank you, **Jim Teets,** for your wonderful thoughts about Ken, your mentor and your friend; and thank you, **Joe Schmieder,** for your thoughts about John and Nancy Kennedy.

I gratefully thank and acknowledge **Dick Lacks, Jr.** for sharing so sensitively the memory of his father and grandfather and the story of the Richard J. Lacks, Sr. Cancer Center and to his mother, the indomitable and dear **Jane Lacks**. Theirs is a lasting tribute to an often tender remembrance. The Lacks family remains one of Saint Mary's true and enduring friends and benefactors. Thank you for your inspired journey with us and for us.

Thank you to **Dr. Bill Passinault** for remembering days gone by and for the legacy you have left us; many thanks to **Terry Moore** and **Russ Visner** for filling in the blanks about the kid from Pewamo—their friend, Mike Jandernoa.

I thank photographer **Hoyt Carrier** for his sensitive visual treatment of our subjects in the book, for his anthology of wonderful images and their scale for this project. And I acknowledge the incomparable **Susan Lovell** for her unselfish sharing of our chief angel, Peter Wege, who once heard the bells ring and got his wings. Where would Saint Mary's be without Peter and his selfless and kind giving ways?

And there are others to thank—from an unsung librarian in Mystic, Connecticut to a retired teacher in Newburyport, Massachusetts, to long-distance editors in Arlington, Virginia and Traverse City, Michigan. I acknowledge them as well.

Throughout this book Mike and I have called upon some of the great sages of history and quoted generously from authors, poets, philosophers and entertainers, some living, others long gone. You will find them listed in the References section. From Thoreau, Eisenhower, Cicero, John Cougar Mellencamp, to Mark Twain and John Wooden, I thank them, too, for their unknowing contributions and for their witticisms and their deep thoughts.

Finally, thank you to *Arbutus Press*, our publisher who has taken all the pieces and parts of this project and turned them into something special, indeed. Without our publisher, there would be no book. So thank you, **Susan Bays**, and your staff for producing *On the Wings of Angels.*

I thank and acknowledge all of the aforementioned people and more, and each of the angels in his or her own right, for their contributions. I owe them my profound gratitude. My greatest fear is that I have forgotten someone. Even in my oversight and errors of omission, there is acknowledgment. Everyone who touched this project should know that.

I hope and pray that this book will be a small part of my indebtedness to Saint Mary's, for my time with all of you, for the best days of my life. If there were no you, there would be no garden to walk through. We are all blessed to embrace Saint Mary's Health Care as we do, one flower, one memory, one patient, one family, one colleague at a time. And so as we go forward together, each in our own separate way, each on our own path, together, forever, I thank you.

Preface

"There is no quality I would rather have and be thought to have than gratitude, for it is not only the greatest virtue but the mother of all the rest."

- Cicero

When I arrived at Saint Mary's in the spring of 2000 the downtown campus looked much different than it does today. The original hospital building at the corner of Cherry and Lafayette that dated back to the late 1800's had served the community well; it had stood the test of time. But like everything else, it had changed; Grand Rapids had changed too—from its cityscape to its grand vision.

But then and now, one thing has never changed: a universal sense of *gratitude* that touches everyone who comes and goes through Saint Mary's doors—from our skilled healers to our gifted staff, from the sick and the injured to anxious and thankful families and friends, and to our generous supporters.

Occasionally, people write thankful letters to the hospital management. Their experience with us validates our mission which says, in part, that Saint Mary's Health Care is here in the spirit of the Gospel, *to heal body, mind and spirit.* People are grateful; their gratitude is like a collective prayer. True, they could go elsewhere, but Saint Mary's is their hospital of choice, and for our physicians and staff, it is an esteemed place to work. Above all, Saint Mary's is a trusted and respected voice that advances health care as a social right in our community. That means something. It sets

Saint Mary's and Catholic health care apart. It defines the integrity
of our institution. So it's not surprising that people have come to
"expect something more." That has become our mantra. Based
on the letters we receive, patients, families and visitors are rarely
disappointed.

*"Dear Saint Mary's Hospital: From the moment I entered
my room until the time I was discharged, I received the most professional and excellent care of any hospital visit I have ever experienced. As busy as I know the staff must have been, they always
treated me as if I was their only patient. I know my family felt the
same way. So often we go through life not appreciating what we
have, especially good health. I am going to tell everyone that if
they need to go into a hospital, to be sure to check out your fine
institution. With renewed health, I say thank you to everyone at
Saint Mary's Hospital."*

The heart of gratitude beats on and on. How do you exit an organization you love? How do you leave a career? How do you thank
the people who have been important to you along your journey?
With my approaching retirement from Saint Mary's and Trinity
Health, I have thought about how to express my gratitude and how
to live my life through my thankfulness. The result is this book. It
is like a nostalgic wave goodbye, a sincere farewell— an expression of my deepest appreciation to everyone who has touched my
life at Saint Mary's and Trinity Health in great and small ways.
And there are many I need to thank.

I titled this book *On the Wings of Angels* because I have
been inspired and nurtured by an angelic presence in my life and in
my work. I have been lifted up by sung and unsung heroes, angels

who support our mission here to "heal body, mind and spirit, to improve the health of our communities and to steward the resources entrusted to us."

Grand Rapids owes its success, in part, to an array of angels in this city. And there are heavenly hosts at Saint Mary's, too. Each and every day, they guide us toward the common good and what is most important. There is angelic love in this special place; our angels are messengers of the Lord who carry out His assignments, who use goodness for God's divine ends. Where would Saint Mary's be without its multitude of angels among us? There are too many to name and recognize in this book, but I would be remiss not to mention a few:

I am grateful to **Sister Mary Maurita Sengelaub**. She has been my mentor and my friend who shined a light on Catholic health care and the healing ministry of Jesus Christ. She helped illuminate the path that I would follow.

I am grateful to **Ralph Hauenstein** – for his generosity, for his kindness and for his vision. Saint Mary's and our community would be a lesser place without him.

I am grateful to **Peter Wege** – for his endless loyalty, for his vast knowledge and for the great lesson he taught me: that held close in the arms of God, it is the good earth that sustains us all, and we must protect it.

I am grateful to **Mike Jandernoa** – for his effective leadership, his invaluable, sincere counsel, and his zeal for the role faith-based health care plays in our community.

I am grateful to the **Lacks family** – for their hearts of gold, for their business savvy and for helping to shape the future of Saint Mary's Heath Care.

I am grateful to **John Canepa** – who always made room for us in his grand vision for Grand Rapids. In celebrating our city and Saint Mary's, we celebrate him.

I am grateful to **Bishop Walter Hurley** – for his leadership across the Diocese of Grand Rapids, for his comradeship and for his embrace of Saint Mary's as the healing arm of the religious flock he leads.

I am grateful to **Dr. Paul Farr** – for the indispensable role he has played with the Saint Mary's Foundation, for his role as an advisor and for his close friendship.

I am grateful to **Ken Hungerford** – for his ability to see and manage the future and for his skill at teaching us how to plan strategically for tomorrow.

I am grateful to **Bob Herr** – for his innate sense of duty and loyalty, for his mentorship, his reliability and for his proven leadership in our community.

I am grateful to **John Kennedy** – for his inspiration and his wonderful logical no-nonsense view of what is needed and how to achieve it; and to **Nancy Kennedy** – for her dedication, spiritual presence, enthusiasm and steadfast commitment to our cause.

And I am grateful to the late **Bishop Kevin Britt** – for always being there while he was with us, for showing me the Catholic way, and for making a difference in my life.

Finally, I am grateful to Trinity Health—one of the largest Catholic health care systems in the country, responsible for running nearly 50 acute care hospitals across America, including Saint Mary's. Trinity Health has been our leader and our inspiration.

People have said that I am the most Catholic non-Catholic they have ever met! As a practicing Episcopalian, I understand how intimately the two faiths are aligned. I hold the Catholic

Church close to my heart. It is a profound theology. It is not a casual faith. And when it comes to health care, Saint Mary's reflects the Church's health care mission and its charge – *to reach out to the afflicted, the distressed and the underserved through the healing ministry of Jesus Christ and in the spirit of the Gospel.*

December 5, 2011 will always be one of the highlights of my life and my career. There in the great expanse of the Cathedral of Saint Andrew in downtown Grand Rapids, before hundreds of well-wishers and devout Catholics from across the Diocese, Bishop Walter Hurley bestowed upon me the *Benemerenti* Medal. It was a Papal honor of the highest rank, a good merit award, first presented by Pope Pius VI, given to a deserving person who has shown exemplary service to the church, family and community. It was a touching and humbling moment that I will treasure always.

Beneath the grand-domed and vaulted ceiling with its many golden stars and hues of blue, with the scent of incense wafting upward and outward amidst the looming clouds of a household of angels, Bishop Hurley spoke about the significance of Catholic health care and our hospital in Grand Rapids.

"If you look out the front door of the Cathedral," said Hurley, "there is, between the Cathedral and Secchia Plaza, a walkway that leads to the front door of Saint Mary's Hospital. That pathway is more than a physical pathway," Hurley continued, "It represents the back-and-forth, the wonderful collaborative relationship that we have with Saint Mary's Hospital."

And with that, Bishop Hurley bestowed upon me the *Benemerenti* Medal. "I am pleased," he said, "to confer, in the name of Pope Benedict XVI, this *Benemerenti* Medal, and I do so with a grateful and thankful heart." It was a moment come and gone in an instant that I will never forget.

Indeed, we are blessed to live and work in a prosperous community. In fact, Grand Rapids is one of the most generous and philanthropic cities in the United States. And Kent County's most pervasive faith? No, it is not Christian Reformed or Reformed. It is Catholic; and so Saint Mary's and Trinity Health play vital roles in our community and for the people we serve. What an honor it has been to lead this organization from which I now take my leave.

Surely, wisdom is rooted in the past. There is comfort in what has gone before. There are lessons I have learned. My father was a career military officer, my mother, a stay-at-home mom. We lived and moved all over the world – from the fascination of Japan to the charm of Paris and across America. It was a wonderful experience. Military life, and later a tour in Vietnam, taught me so much about order, the chain of command, what to expect, how to behave, what to do and what not to do, and the value of humility over egotism.

At Wake Forest University I took a course in hospital administration. I was hooked! My brother, who became a neurosurgeon, and I worked summers in hospitals, so health care became an obvious pursuit. I studied management at The George Washington University and discovered I loved the business and finance side as much as the clinical and patient care. After a residency at the Baptist Hospital in Jacksonville, Florida and my first administrative job in South Carolina, with an exposure to rural health care, I set my sights on a larger urban facility. I was one of 300 applicants who applied to help lead Butterworth Hospital. I got the job, came to Grand Rapids in 1975 and stayed on the hill for 25 years. With the creation of Spectrum Health in 1997, I eventually left the organization and moved on in 1999.

In retrospect my post-Butterworth job search over the next nine months was a remarkable odyssey. Later I would look back on my journey and understand what my confidant, Bishop Robert J. Rose, always told me—that we are "called" to do the work that we do. Now I know what he meant and that, truly, God has a plan for us. He certainly had a plan for me.

The journey that led me to Saint Mary's was an essential time in my life. It included consulting assignments in Great Falls, Montana and missionary work in Croatia with Mercy International Health Services. Little did I know that I was being groomed to stay in Grand Rapids, to be in a Catholic community and a fixture in faith-based health care. It was all part of God's plan.

That plan included a chance encounter with a most special angel—Sister Mary Maurita Sengelaub. You will meet her in the first chapter of this book. Without her guidance and counsel, I would not have landed where I did. She remains one of the dearest people in my life; she taught me what it means to be Catholic and what Catholic health care is all about.

Yesterday and today, Grand Rapids remains a vital community with a wonderful medical and health care outreach story. So it was not surprising that I chose to come here and stay here. This is a good place with remarkable people who practice generosity and gratitude in their daily lives.

Driving from my home in Cascade to my downtown office has been a wonderful ritual over the years. Indeed, life follows the seasons across West Michigan. The landmarks have changed but the route to and from Saint Mary's is indelible. Looking out my office window, I have the best view in town! I can see the cross atop the Cathedral of Saint Andrew. Sometimes against the rising sun and a purple sky, it sparkles like solid gold. With glowing colors of gleaming chrome, the cross never disappoints me. When I see it, I know it's going to be a good day, a very good day.

There is nothing more gratifying than to walk the halls of Saint Mary's and feel the pulse of this place. It is like a city alive. The heart beats and the energy flows. You can sense it and feel its beat—from the greeters in the lobby to the cafeteria cashiers, from the patient care units to the radiology suites—in genuine smiles and in sincere hand shakes. Everywhere and every day we count on our staff to do their very best work, to be the hospital's face and its warm embrace. How rewarding for a chief executive to see that in action and to leave it now with such a positive well-oiled model in place.

Over the course of its existence, Saint Mary's has evolved just like its name—from Saint Mary's Hospital, to Saint Mary's Health Services, to Saint Mary's Mercy Medical Center to Saint Mary's Health Care. After an extensive identity study, in the summer of 2004, we rolled out our new name–Saint Mary's Health Care. We wanted to re-introduce ourselves as not just the hospital on Jefferson Avenue but as the hospital system that delivered excellent medical care with individualized attention.

I always saw myself as a facilitator—helping other people do their jobs so they can serve our patients and their families with empathy, sensitivity and skill. Saint Mary's is much more than bricks and mortar, much more than a place where we simply come to work. It is all about the people inside. I see them every day. They lift me up. I would not be where I am, and who I am, without all of the angels in my life, without all of you.

Early on, Saint Mary's designed a strategy to transform the hospital from what it was to what it could become—from a traditional predictable place to a grand and preeminent institution, a place where people come because they "expect something more," and they receive it; today we deliver on that promise. We earn people's business and their trust because we know they can choose to go someplace else. That vision included re-focusing our services, from primary care to high technology to advanced cancer treatment to innovative neuroscience services, to community clinics and environmentally friendly new buildings. Over time, Saint Mary's has become more than simply an option to the hospital down the street; for those who come here, it has become their hospital of choice. That was my dream for this place. And there is more work to do.

Since I came to Saint Mary's in 2000, the image has changed. And thanks to our generous supporters, our angels, the hospital itself has changed too. Look around today and you will see impressive centers of excellence: the Richard J. Lacks, Sr. Cancer Center; the Hauenstein Neuroscience Center; and Sophia's House. We have introduced and implemented electronic health records, LEED-certified buildings; and so much more. It all adds up to define Saint Mary's as an advanced health care facility.

But what has never changed is the *soul* of this place – our willingness to care for patients regardless of who you are or where you come from, to hold close the underserved, to exercise kindness, concern and respect with a sense of social justice. Those are core values that mean something. And so in these times of historic health care reform, Saint Mary's is more important than ever within our caring community.

We are a healing ministry of Jesus Christ. That is undeniable. We are "called" to do the work that we do. We are part of God's plan and his family. Indeed, there are angels among us, many who are often in disguise. And there is extreme gratitude—

knowing that a single grateful thought is the most complete prayer. With fond memories and love, that is what I leave you—the simplest form of gratitude: a thankful heart!

Philip H. McCorkle Jr.
Grand Rapids, Michigan
June 2013

PREFACE

A Messenger From God

Sister Mary Maurita Sengelaub

"God not only sends special angels into our lives, but sometimes He even sends them back again if we forget to take notes the first time."

-The Angels' Little Instruction Book

If I forget everything that I have ever learned—I will always remember Sister Mary Maurita Sengelaub. She is my mentor, my teacher and my friend. I often wonder what might have become of me had this treasured "angel" with her sage advice and gentle heart not come into my life when and how she did. Indeed, Sister Maurita was an angelic messenger from God, part of His plan for me, and an answer to my prayers.

1995 was a watershed year: gas cost $1.09 a gallon; Windows 95 was released; the OJ trial finally ended; The Grateful Dead announced their break-up; Bill Clinton was president. A year earlier discussions had begun about the creation of Spectrum Health. The genesis of merging Grand Rapids' two largest hospitals was at hand. I would be one of its architects. Butterworth Hospital, where I had worked since 1975, and Blodgett Memorial Medical Center would play central roles in the evolution of a vast new amalgamated health care system across West Michigan. At the time, there was anxiety in the hospital hallways and angst in my office, too, where I served Butterworth as its CEO. Would I be a player in the co-mingled system or a casualty? Would I leave the organization or would it leave me?

Chance encounters and close relationships are at the core of how business often happens in Grand Rapids. Someone knows somebody who knows somebody. It is part of the city's gene pool —building a close association with a good friend or a trusted colleague. One thing leads to another. People talk. Things work out. Deals are done, often quietly under the radar. Life just happens. And so the best advice is invariably to "just go with it, see where this takes you." Call it good fortune, providence or destiny; I call it God's plan. And so between 1995 and 2000, I just "went with it." Living and working day to day was like a moving current; life simply swept me along. But I had no idea where God's plan was taking me or what I would be doing for the rest of my life, or where.

In the spring of 1999, events were tenuous at the new and still evolving Spectrum Health. But the handwriting was on the wall. It was time to move on and find an institution that fit my values. I left Butterworth Hospital and began a most amazing and unexpected journey, a fascinating odyssey. It was an emotional leave-taking – to exit an organization that I loved, to say goodbye to people I cherished. But in time, unknowingly, the puzzle pieces in God's plan for me started to fit together.

Many of my dearest friends were fellow congregants at Grand Rapids' Grace Episcopal Church where I worshiped. By now the situation at Spectrum Health was common knowledge, that I had left Butterworth and was exploring new opportunities. I started talking to people, doing my research, making phone calls, reaching out, planning the rest of my life. My journey started with a most fortunate encounter with a church member whose husband's sister had gone to nursing school with a woman named Mary Maurita Sengelaub. "Do you know her? She might be able to help you. You must meet her!" And so it began–bumping into an acquaintance at my church, someone who knew somebody who knew somebody. Was I simply at the right place at the right time, or was this Divine intervention?

When I first called Sister Maurita, I learned that she was in the infirmary at the McAuley Center in Farmington Hills recovering from a stress fracture to her foot. She had recently retired from Mercy Health Services and had once served Saint Mary's Hospital as its administrator in the late 1950s. After a short recovery and her return to Grand Rapids, we agreed to meet.

Our first encounter was over lunch at Charley's Crab, one of Sister Maurita's favorite Grand Rapids restaurants. I picked her up at Saint Mary's front entrance, and we drove the short distance for our meeting. We sat at a secluded table overlooking the Grand River, a relaxed setting for a private conversation that would lead to more lunches, absorbing dialogue, and useful advice. Sister Maurita was a special angel: caring, gentle, warm-hearted, a true Samaritan, a brilliant teacher and a gifted administrator; there was no one in America who knew more about Catholic health care, and I had a lot to learn. She wore a navy blue business suit with a spotlessly pressed white lace collar. Her graying coiffured hair was immaculately combed just so. Large round glasses framed her face and magnified the twinkle in her eye. And there was that disarming smile. She talked and I listened, giving credence to why God gave us two ears and one mouth.

Faith-based hospitals were foreign territory for me. At Spectrum Health, with such a diverse patient and employee base, the spiritual side of healing was not a primary focus. On the other hand, with Catholic health care, it was. Sister Maurita explained to me that hospitals like Saint Mary's were all about the "ministry of healing" and, above all else, they seek to "treat people with great tenderness, compassion and the love of God." Catholic hospitals, she said, existed to carry out the mission of the church and nurture the dignity of the whole person—because "we are all created in His likeness." Above all, Catholic health care stressed justice and morality – doing what is right and what is true for everyone, including the poor and the underserved. How could I not want to be involved with such a noble and virtuous mission?

At that first Charley's Crab lunch, Sister Maurita knew more about me than I knew about her. She was familiar with my situation; she had heard the buzz around town – that I was kicking the health care tires to find the right fit. Sister Maurita was a mover and shaker. She knew everyone in town, whom to talk to, where to go and where all the bodies were buried. And she knew that Saint Mary's was looking for a new CEO. The timing was right. "Did I have an interest?" She suggested I learn as much as I could, and that I should plan to visit the headquarters of Mercy Health Services in Farmington Hills. My education was at hand.

More lunches followed our first meeting: the 1913 Room Restaurant at the Amway Grand Plaza Hotel and back to Charley's Crab. I was in the presence of a giant in the industry. Sister Maurita had been a major Catholic health care pioneer on two continents over six decades. She was a nurse before she was a sister, but she was always an educator and a world traveler. "Throughout my life," she later wrote, "I have been invited to do new things, and I have enjoyed many different opportunities to serve people. I learned that the most important thing is to carry with you each day the love of God and the love of others."

Sister Maurita moved in the right circles. She had worked tirelessly for the underserved in New York City, Detroit, Washington, D.C. and even in far-off Perth, Australia with the Sisters of St. John of God. For seven years, Sister Maurita served the Catholic Health Association (CHA) as its Executive Director, a position that made a lasting impact on other health care systems across the nation and around the world.

Born in 1918, Sister Maurita is a survivor. After enduring three bouts with cancer, lingering heart disease and osteoporosis, she remains strong and keen and determined, yet gentle, just like an angel. While illness may have drained her vitality, it did not diminish her drive. A devout follower of Jesus, Sister Maurita is also a passionate devotee of the venerable Catherine McAuley, founder of the Sisters of Mercy whose organization is devoted to living, caring, humility, meekness, listening, encouraging and enabling others. McAuley's virtues set the standard for Catholic health care around the world, and Sister Maurita became a true and faithful servant.

Coincidentally, the Mercy International office in Farmington Hills was planning a missionary trip to Croatia. Did I want to go? Sister Maurita encouraged me to make the trip, to consult, to do a study and write a report. It turned out to be a monumental experience that provided me with a firsthand look at Catholic health care on a global scale. After my experience in Croatia, I traveled to Great Falls, Montana to consult in a community with a Catholic hospital. It was all part of the education of Phil McCorkle. Was God preparing me for a larger job?

Sister Maurita helped me focus. Using Croatia and Great Falls as measures of my interest, I came to realize that my true love and my passion was to work with people in a spiritual setting and in a caring community, a setting like Saint Mary's Health Care with its profound healing ministry of Jesus Christ, and in Grand Rapids, a city of faith, with its highly-regarded medical reputation. Sister Maurita recognized that I was a man of reflection and prayer, and that I was committed to doing the right thing. The Saint Mary's CEO position seemed like the right fit. Was I ready for a Catholic hospital?

My experiences in Great Falls and Croatia convinced me that Catholic health care would be my life's work. Catherine McAuley's mission, and the origins of Mercy Health Services (a forerunner of Trinity Health), combined with Sister Maurita's counsel, guidance and encouragement, became an inspiration. My mind was made up. There was no turning back now.

At one of our lunches, Sister Maurita suggested several books that I might want to read. One of those books that I still treasure today is *Jesus CEO: Using Ancient Wisdom for Visionary Leadership* by Laurie Beth Jones. Jones' book is a practical corporate tutorial for communicating with and motivating people. It is based on the self-mastery, action, and relationship skills Jesus used to train and inspire his followers and how He harnessed spiritual energy to empower his disciples. Jones writes that Jesus did not waste his time judging others. He spent his energy creating and supporting. Jesus gave people a vision of something larger than themselves. "Follow me," Jesus said, "and you will never be thirsty again." And Jesus was not a low-profile person. He was visible. He had a passionate commitment to the cause. He took the long view. He had a plan. He formed a team. He called the question. I highly recommend the book to anyone in the administration or management field. It will change one's view of how to manage, relate, and motivate people.

Over time Sister Maurita became convinced that I was the right person for Saint Mary's Health Care, that this was where I belonged, that I was the one who would best "safeguard the assets of the hospital." It was part of my spiritual journey to be at this place at this time. So she encouraged me to apply for the CEO position explaining that as part of God's plan, I was called to this ministry. I threw my hat in the ring; I made the cut from a dozen applicants to five to three to one. And I was the one! I was quoted in *The Grand Rapids Press*, that "it was the time of my life, that I was on a mission from God."

Catholic health care fulfills a special mission in the church – to be trusted partners in improving community health for everyone, including the poor and the underserved. In my studies and in my meditation, Matthew 25 seemed to say it all: "For I was hungry and you gave me food, I was thirsty and you gave me drink, I was a stranger and you welcomed me, I was naked and you clothed me, I was sick and you visited me, I was in prison and you came to me." As Saint Mary's new President and CEO, it defined our mission and my values.

On June 21, 2000 a formal commissioning ceremony was held in my honor at the Cathedral of Saint Andrew in Grand Rapids. It was only the second such celebration for a new President and CEO in the hospital's long history. What a profound moment. I could only think of three other events that had made such an impact on my life: my marriage to Gayle and the birth of our two sons. "Two hundred friends and family, hospital staff and donors prayed for McCorkle's success," *The Grand Rapids Press* reported the following day.

Gothic in architecture, the Cathedral of Saint Andrew dates back to 1850. It is one of the city's most sacred buildings with vaulted ceilings and pillars, gold leaf, decorative marble, ceramic wainscot, tiled floors, glorious stained glass windows, a maple and granite altar, and a world-class organ.

The Cathedral provided an overwhelming setting for the ceremony, like none I had ever experienced. It was as moving and humbling as it was spiritual: magnificent music (a collaboration between the music departments of the Cathedral and Grace Episcopal Church where I served as a Lay Eucharistic Minister); moving evening prayers; liturgical dance; comments by the Right Reverend Edward L. Lee, Jr. (Bishop of the Episcopal Diocese of Western Michigan); and by the Most Reverend Robert J. Rose (Bishop of the Diocese of Grand Rapids). Before my family, before old and new friends, before colleagues and before God, I promised to uphold the Trinity Health mission: *"We serve together in Trinity Health in the spirit of the Gospel, to heal body, mind, and spirit, to improve the health of our communities, and to steward the resources entrusted to us."*

"During my life, I have had wonderful jobs," I wrote, "But never before have I had the opportunity to be an integral part of such a profound ministry. I am deeply grateful for these blessings and for your support."

Central to the ceremony was a special reading by my friend, Sister Maurita. I wanted an angelic presence to be part of my commissioning. She read from I John 5: "Every one who believes that Jesus is the Christ is a child of God, and every one who loves the parent loves the child. By this we know that we love the children of God, when we love God and obey His commandments. For this is the love of God, that we keep His commandments. And

His commandments are not burdensome. For whatever is born of God overcomes the world; and this is the victory that overcomes the world, our faith. Who is it that overcomes the world but he who believes that Jesus is the Son of God?"

Sister Maurita's scripture reading—that we are all children of God – still rings true. In the ensuing days, weeks, months and years as President and CEO of Saint Mary's Health Care, I found the words continued to resonate—that the victory that overcomes the world is our faith. When I think about being a child of God, I think about my friend, Sister Maurita.

In 2005 Sister Maurita celebrated her Jubilee with the Sisters of Mercy of the Americas. It meant a lot to her and to me, because she was my special angel. "It is a celebration of a life fulfilled with untold blessings, graces, surprises and awe while journeying with the Triune God these past sixty years," she wrote. "God's gifts have energized and supported me in my relationship with family, friends, benefactors, Sisters of Mercy, colleagues and co-workers in service to the people of God. It is being celebrated with tremendous gratitude, deepest love, great joy and an everlasting commitment to God's call."

Indeed, we are called to do the Lord's work on earth. The people we meet along the way, often angels in disguise, like Sister Maurita, do not come into our lives simply by chance. They are messengers from God. They come in all forms, visible and invisible, apparent or subtle. They may be powerful images or humble servants – an inconspicuous man or a simple woman in a navy blue business suit with a pressed lace collar. With their presence, they leave us with wonderful memories and the fruits of their charity. Most of all, the angels in our lives leave us with hope as we carry on in joy and renewal.

The Wind Behind My Back

Ralph W. Hauenstein

"Leadership is the art of getting someone else to do something you want done because he wants to do it."
-Dwight D. Eisenhower

Celebrated writers far more imaginative than I, like Joseph Campbell or the prolific Greek poet Pindar, have written that "the beauty of an aged face is like a white candle in a holy place," and "that a graceful old age is the childhood of immortality," or from Longfellow, that "to be seventy years old is like climbing the Alps!" What, then, would the sage philosophers say about Ralph Hauenstein en route to 102 and beyond? I pray that he sticks around long enough to read these words. I think he will. Angels are ageless, after all.

In February 2009 Saint Mary's Health Care formally opened the Hauenstein Neuroscience Center, one of the most remarkable and advanced facilities of its kind in America, and located right here in Grand Rapids. Not only is it a tribute to the research and treatment of vexing neurological afflictions such as ALS, Alzheimer's, Parkinson's, epilepsy, acute stroke, and other disorders, but it also honors its staff and the selfless exemplar whose name it bears – Ralph W. Hauenstein.

While the story of how the Hauenstein Neuroscience Center evolved and came to be is noteworthy, the epic narrative of Ralph Hauenstein's life and times is a monumental American experience. Without the military brain trust of the many who helped plan the strategy that triumphed over Nazi Germany, World War II in Europe might have ended very differently. Today, we could be singing a different national anthem had it not been for the courage and skill of soldier-leaders like Colonel Hauenstein.

I first met him in 1995 during the formative years of the Van Andel Institute where Ralph was an initial trustee when I was CEO at Butterworth Hospital. The early evolution of what would become Spectrum Health was at hand and so was the Van Andel Research Institute. Butterworth and the VAI would form a close association as we gathered to cement our partnership, focus on its future and honor its benefactors – Jay and Betty Van Andel. Ralph was younger then, only 83. I didn't know who he was, this modest man who radiated an easy friendship I would come to treasure. Other than exchanging brief hellos and cordial small talk, it was an uneventful first encounter.

Six years later, after I had landed at Saint Mary's, Ralph was admitted to the hospital with chronic bronchitis. As the new CEO, it was my custom to walk the halls from time to time and drop in unexpectedly to greet newly admitted patients. It was part of my ministry at the institution I had come to love. There was Ralph sitting up in bed looking quite chipper and in good spirits, wearing official hospital garb, resting comfortably and appearing remarkably younger than his 89 years. I had no idea that he was such a celebrated citizen and one of Grand Rapids' most generous philanthropists. We chatted casually, like old friends. "Is there anything I can do for you?" I asked. In a raspy almost hoarse voice, he answered my question with a question that I will never forget: "Is there anything I can do for you?" with an emphasis on you, Saint Mary's. It was not the answer I expected, and I didn't know how to react. Little did I know that my courtesy call on Ralph was the genesis of what would become Saint Mary's Hauenstein Neuroscience Center.

To fully appreciate Ralph Hauenstein, it's important to know his background and his story. He was born in Fort Wayne, Indiana in 1912 and moved to Grand Rapids when he was a young boy. Michigan became his adoptive home. When he was 23 he was commissioned into the U.S. Army Reserve as a Second Lieutenant and became a commander of an all African-American Civilian Conservation Corps camp. Two and a half years later, Ralph returned home and became city editor of *The Grand Rapids Herald,* whose former publisher and editor was once the legendary and revered Senator Arthur H. Vandenberg.

A year before Pearl Harbor, Ralph returned to active duty in the Army and eventually rose to the rank of Colonel. He is a proud member of what historians call "The Greatest Generation." During World War II, from late 1943 until the summer of 1945, Ralph worked in Intelligence. Assigned to the European Theater of Operations, he was one of the phantoms of the Army's war effort, rising to Chief of Intelligence Branch (G-2) Hq. European Theater of Operations U.S. Army. He was a key player for the Allies and for the Supreme Headquarters Allied Expeditionary Forces where he worked closely with General Dwight Eisenhower. Colonel Hauenstein helped plan the D-Day invasion in June 1944; he led a team of code-breakers throughout Europe, who were critical to the Allied victory. As the war neared an end, Ralph helped free Paris from Nazi occupation, and he was one of the liberators of the Dachau concentration camp. He had seen and experienced the horrors of inhumanity and atrocity and was awarded for his service with the Legion of Merit, the Bronze Star, the European Eastern Service Medal, and the Order of the British Empire from the United Kingdom. In 2012 Hauenstein was awarded the French Legion of Honor.

After the war, he returned home to Grand Rapids with a new sense of duty, a far-sighted commitment to his community and a desire and determination that drove his patriotic ideals. The war had made a lasting impression on Ralph, and he resolved to work for positive international relations and peaceful solutions to conflict. "Anything is possible," became his mantra, and making the world a better place became his passion.

From his home base in Grand Rapids, Hauenstein pursued a business career in global trade. He partnered with enterprises in Europe and the Middle East to provide products and services to consumers abroad and to struggling democracies. I learned that Ralph is a risk taker; he underwrote the cost of a modern bakery in Haiti that provided jobs for hundreds of workers and thousands of individual distributors at a difficult time in the island country's history of poverty and hardship. He also started a school in Florida that taught destitute people from developing countries how to run a fully automated bakery that provided good jobs for the local economy. He was a true humanitarian with a charitable heart.

The more I got to know him, the more I became acquainted with his life and his story. He and his wife Grace were strong Catholics. Ralph once served the Second Vatican Council in Rome as a consultant, and his wife's aunt, Sister Mary Grace, worked as an administrator at Saint Mary's. So there was a strong attraction to us, and it is no wonder that Ralph's wife always called Saint Mary's "my hospital."

So there lay Ralph Hauenstein in Room 632 with an an-
noying cough and chronic bronchitis, but also with a heart of gold
and a Rolodex full of friends and associates who owed him favors.
As Ralph shared his affection for Saint Mary's, I learned that his
father, Leon Hauenstein, had been afflicted with, and later died
of, Parkinson's disease. In 2008 Grace succumbed to the ravages
of Alzheimer's, so it was understandable that there was a such a
strong bond to our hospital and to the pursuits of neuroscience.
And there was Ralph's good friend, Jay Van Andel, who also suffered from Parkinson's. The disease would eventually take him in
2004; Jay's dear wife Betty would die from Alzheimer's the same
year. It was a rare convergence of circumstances that created the
critical mass necessary to plant and grow what we know today as
the Hauenstein Neuroscience Center at Saint Mary's.

Timing can be a very paradoxical force; or is it simply
God's plan working itself out and through our lives? You see,
shortly after I started working at Saint Mary's, the Parkinson's Association approached me asking if we had space on our campus to
develop a clinic for Parkinson's patients. Saint Mary's had already
identified neuroscience as an unmet need in the community, and
so it seemed like a reasonable request at the time. It would require
some renovation to accommodate exam and consultation rooms.
And so the answer was, yes, we would be willing to make it happen. But how? And where would the money come from?

I thought back on Ralph's offer after our first encounter
in his hospital room: "Is there anything I can do for you?" I'll
always remember him asking me the question. Well, here was
something he could, indeed, do for us. And so I talked to Ralph
about the request from the Parkinson's Association. He liked the
idea. Once the details for the clinic had been worked out, Ralph

made a few phone calls. Quietly – and with little fanfare – the initial money was raised. This was thanks, in part, to Ralph and his cadre of friends. The renovation took place during the summer and in October of 2003, the space was formally dedicated. Ralph seemed a bit perplexed as he looked around during the ceremonial gathering of dignitaries. He whispered to me that he thought the space was much too small, that we were going to need a much larger facility. Ralph was not someone you disagreed with, and so I concurred with his observation. "Well, yes, Ralph you have a good point. You're probably right. The space is too small," I said. Thus, the seeds were planted to create a far more expansive facility that would serve a growing number of people with Parkinson's and brain and spine-related afflictions; and to help care for and nurture them and their families.

Ralph was a big thinker. Anyone who was involved in planning the D-Day Invasion during WWII would have to be. His vision for Saint Mary's was broad and deep. So was mine. Initially, Ralph had to hold me down and temper my dreams, but in the end, his ambitions became as far-reaching as my own. It was inspiring, so much so that it motivated Saint Mary's to envision a wider, more expansive facility than the modest space that had just been dedicated. Strategically, we would play to our strengths and to our centers of excellence: oncology, orthopedics, primary care, and now, neuroscience. Initially it was a modest proposal, but after we discussed the greater need, we realized that a much more profound response would position us better. We thought in terms of one large umbrella under which would emerge a new emergency and trauma department, an intensive care and a critical care unit, offices and a modern clinic space necessary to treat patients with neurological diseases. A multi-level parking garage was part of the plan as well. We were excited; so was Trinity Health. Never in its history would a project so unique gain approval so fast. And as it evolved, the money came, too, not only from Trinity Health, but from the community and Saint Mary's staff—small and large donations, from a diverse cross section of supporters. The entire project was estimated to cost $60 million. We needed to raise $15 million. Thanks to Ralph, that goal was realized. $3 million came from Ralph himself. Eventually, his personal donations will continue. And through his connections and the power of his relationships and his name in the community, through his phone calls and arm twisting, Ralph personally got us in the door. He was there for the takeoff and he would be there for the landing, too. Saint Mary's could not have asked for a more bighearted friend or giving benefactor. Indeed, Ralph is the wind behind my back and the force behind the hospital's neuroscience dreams. He is our special angel.

As plans for the new center began to take shape, Ralph and I formed a strong bond and a lasting friendship. In 2005 my parents came to visit me in Grand Rapids. My father was a retired WWII Army officer, and I thought he and Ralph would enjoy each other's company. I asked Ralph if he would like to join us at the Peninsular Club. He and my father, Colonel Hauenstein and Colonel McCorkle, could talk shop over lunch. Indeed, rank has its privileges. Ralph's book, *Intelligence Was My Line: Inside Eisenhower's Other Command*, had just been published, and I wanted my father to have an autographed copy. My dad and Ralph hit it off and traded war stories over lunch. The encounter really helped personalize our relationship. As time went on, Ralph would always ask about my father, and my father would always ask, "How is Ralph doing?" It had blossomed into a family affair.

My interest in neuroscience and the Hauenstein Center project was not coincidental. My brother, Cavert, is a neurosurgeon in South Carolina; and in my studies and my fascination with medicine, I learned that "the brain is the new heart." So much of medicine had been focused on cardiovascular disease, valve replacement, and heart bypass surgery. But now Saint Mary's neuroscience center would shine its light on the new frontiers of brain and neuromuscular disorders. And there would be strong partnerships with the Van Andel Research Institute and the Michigan State University College of Human Medicine. The Hauenstein Neurosceience Center would become a major asset to the community, to West Michigan, the state and the nation; and to think that its genesis could be traced back to Ralph's pointed question years earlier: "Is there anything I can do for you?"

As the Hauenstein Neuroscience Center evolved and grew brick by brick and dream by dream, Ralph was typically modest about his contribution. He was more than pleased with the Center and the fact that it would incorporate outpatient and inpatient services, a new critical care unit, a new emergency department and a Level II trauma facility, all under one roof. Ralph was particularly pleased that West Michigan patients would no longer have to travel to Chicago, Ann Arbor, the Cleveland Clinic or to the Mayo Clinic for the latest treatment of their neurological disorders.

In December 2008, Ralph's dear wife Grace died from Alzheimer's. Neither she nor Jay and Betty Van Andel would ever see the dedication of the Hauenstein Neuroscience Center that came in late February 2009. But Ralph would. It was a day he will long cherish and remember—a great day for Saint Mary's, for Trinity Health, for Grand Rapids, for West Michigan and the nation.

The fanfare that surrounded the grand opening was surpassed only by the gleam in Ralph's eyes. All of us shared his delight and our gratitude for him. We celebrated our great collective joy and embraced God's blessing upon Saint Mary's Health Care and the angels among us.

From time to time, Ralph would unexpectedly show up at Saint Mary's and walk through the Hauenstein Neurosceience Center, "just to see how things were going and what was going on," he would say. Strolling down the halls became a regular ritual. It was his gladness. "What a pleasure it is to work here," people would tell Ralph. They would greet him and thank him with grateful hugs and handshakes. Everyone knew Ralph. He was as recognizable as the time of day and as timely as the sunrise.

More than anything, the Hauenstein Neurosceience Center reflected Ralph's appreciation for quality and innovation. The fingerprints of those who would work here were everywhere. Case in point: the patient rooms were designed by our own nurses to ensure that they would not only meet the patients' needs but also the needs of the staff who would serve the patients and their families. That had never been done before, and Ralph treasured such a novel approach. "It's a quality place that attracts quality people," he observed.

In September 2009 a unique event was celebrated at the Hauenstein Neuroscience Center. Designed as a LEED-certified facility with a garden and environmentally efficient and spacious enclaves, the Center needed a special touch that would enhance its healing atmosphere. One of the waiting areas had a delightful view of the Center's garden. It needed a therapeutic presence and a "curative spirit" to watch over the Center and the patients and families who would come here. That spirit came in the form of a wonderful statue commissioned by Ralph's children in honor of their father and mother. And so on September 2, 2009, members of the staff and the Hauenstein family gathered to commemorate a sculpture of Saint Raphael. Today, this special likeness of one of our most precious archangels has taken its rightful place in the Center's garden.

Saint Raphael was chosen because he is one of our best loved angels and is recognized across Christianity, Judaism and Islam. Raphael is the Patron Saint of physicians; he is the angel of healing, of science, and the regent of the sun. Sounds a lot like Ralph Hauenstein; perhaps we should call Ralph "Angel Ralpha-el?"

Yes, rank has its privileges. Colonel Hauenstein would not disagree. But as I write this, age also has its privileges. American poet, Rod McKuen, could not have said it more eloquently in his unpublished poem: *Age is better.* He shares that once he had been young, strong and in a rush to be older. Then upon seeing his re-flection, he discovers that he had, in fact, become older. Rod McK-uen observes that "age erases pretense; replacing it with honesty." You get to say what you really think.

And so it goes. *Age is better.* Just ask the Angel "Ralphael."

An Angel Gets His Wings

Peter M. Wege

*"Do all the good you can for as many people
as you can for as long as you can."*

-Peter M. Wege

W hen the bells ring out on Sunday mornings in Grand Rapids' countless church towers, it brings to mind that memorable line in the 1946 classic film, *It's a Wonderful Life:* "When a bell rings, an angel gets his wings." The sound of bells pealing is commonplace here. It is like the voice of God, dependable, predictable and ever-present. We are truly blessed by the sound of all things sacred. And we are blessed by the pioneers who built Grand Rapids, who made this community a better place in which to live and work and recreate, people like Peter M. Wege who, many years ago, heard the bells ring, got his wings and made his presence known like a prophet here. All of us are the beneficiaries of his generosity, his passion and his artful giving. His is a good heart, indeed. And few institutions have received the bounty of his kindness as has Saint Mary's Health Care, confirming the expression that "friendship is a knot tied by an angel's hands."

In 1943 First Lieutenant and transport pilot Peter Wege, then only 23 years old, was delivering an Army Air Force plane from Michigan to West Point, New York. His fate was decreed, ordained by God's plan, and his destiny was assured in a remarkable way. In the light of day, flying east through the black smog over Pittsburgh, Wege could not see the vast city below him. The smoke and the grit and the soot that drifted up from the steel town below, where armaments for the war in Europe and the Pacific were methodically produced, were as thick and dense as midnight. It was a defining moment for Wege, an environmental epiphany, he recalls. The experience of looking down upon an engulfed American city, as dark as a cellar at high noon, made an indelible impression. Conserving and sustaining the earth would become a passion Peter would champion for the rest of his life. Environmental stewardship became one of Wege's Five Pillars that he pursued from the trenches of good causes across Grand Rapids and beyond—education, arts and culture, health care, human services and, of course, the environment.

In the spring of 2000, shortly after I became CEO at Saint Mary's, my plan was to reach out to key influential Catholics in the community. Bishop Robert Rose and Peter Wege headed the list, two of our most effective and influential advocates of all things Catholic across the diocese. They were both steadfast supporters of quality health care in West Michigan. Peter had a celebrated history with the hospital. In fact, he remains the longest sustaining and most generous benefactor we have. Peter has served on the hospital's board; he is a founding trustee of the Saint Mary's Foundation, and he has touched and supported virtually every major project the hospital has proposed and pursued over six decades. In short, Peter Wege is the one! He is at the center of everything!

Peter's roots run deep in Grand Rapids. Born in the winter of 1920, the only child of Peter Martin and Sophia Louise Wege, he made his mark at the company his father helped found, Steelcase, Inc., which evolved into the world's largest manufacturer of office furniture. After serving in North Africa during the war, Peter returned home and joined the organization, working in various capacities until his retirement in 1985. During his tenure, and much to his credit, the company grew and thrived and was influenced by Peter's revolutionary ideas, his creativity, inventiveness, wisdom and vision. In 1968 Peter created his own foundation and became one of the nation's preeminent twentieth-century philanthropists. Today, his selfless tradition of giving, to make the world a better place, continues as Peter lives his motto like a beacon that others might follow: "Do all the good you can for as many people as you can for as long as you can."

Ask Peter Wege to define generosity and he might quote the great newspaper writer, George F. Burba, who said that, "those who give the most have the most left;" he might quote Thoreau, that "if you give money, spend yourself with it," or Belgian cardinal, Desiree Joseph Mercier, that "we must not only give what we have but also give what we are." Wege might even recite a line from one of his own poems, "The beauty of all life is the time you spend with your heart..."

Founded in honor of Peter's loving parents, the Wege Foundation has helped transform Grand Rapids and, in particular, Catholic institutions. His foundation became Peter's vehicle to do charitable business. In addition to Saint Mary's Health Care, Peter has given generously to institutions like Aquinas College, where he is known as the college's best friend, to the Grand Rapids Catholic Diocese, St. Stephen's School and Parish in East Grand Rapids, and the Franciscan Life Process Center in Lowell. Peter is also strongly associated with the arts in Grand Rapids. He was a member of the committee that brought Alexander Calder's sculpture, "La Grande Vitesse," to our city in 1969. Peter helped raise $2.2 million to restore the venerable Wealthy Theater in 1997. He has had a major impact on the Grand Rapids Symphony in its music, its programming and its outreach in the community. In 2001, Peter generously gave the lead gift of $20 million for the construction of Grand Rapids' magnificent downtown art museum. And in 2007 a gift from the Wege Foundation partially funded a marvelous new Grand Rapids Ballet headquarters that officially opened in 2010. And in the realm of human services, Peter has always had a meaningful presence by supporting urban endeavors like Grand Rapids' Dwelling Place, the Heartside neighborhood, and Heartside Ministries, "to help dignify the homeless, the downtrodden and the mentally ill."

In concert with his philanthropic heart is Peter's passion for our planet. His environmental activism is legendary, a commitment he traces back to 1943 and his life-changing flight over Pittsburgh. That singular experience left a heavy mark on his conscience; it helped form his principled thinking and spurred his quest to provide a healthy living experience for all people of the earth. "If we continue to treat our planet as if its supply of sustenance were infinite," he wrote, "we guarantee that our world and all life on it will come to an end."

Peter's zest for the environment was explained in two books he wrote: *Economicology: The Eleventh Commandment,* published in 1998, and *Economicology II,* published in 2010, in which he championed the earth as "a precious and sacred place beyond all comparison or measure." Peter wrote that "we are all one family under God. We are one ecosystem and one planet in an infinity of space and time. It is our home, and we can no longer sweep mankind's destructive ways under our environmental rug." He has spent most of his adult life dedicated to making right what people in the world have made wrong—from overpopulation to saving the Great Lakes and much more.

In all the years I had lived and worked in Grand Rapids, I had never met Peter Wege. And so in the spring of 2000, shortly after arriving at Saint Mary's as the hospital's new CEO, I went to visit him at his home in East Grand Rapids that overlooks idyllic Reeds Lake. It seemed that he was as eager to meet me as I was to meet him. Peter greeted me with a firm handshake and a beaming smile that lit up his round face. We sat and chatted and began a close friendship. He was easy to read. He was trusting and supportive. He was a deep forward thinker. He was a challenging prophetic voice in Grand Rapids. And he was a life-long learner who was ahead of his time. Above all, he loved the Catholic faith and Saint Mary's Health Care.

Peter had been a major force at Saint Mary's long before our first meeting. His vision preceded my dream to turn the hospital into a renowned health care institution. It seemed that every time he and I sat down, Peter would lead with the same question: "Do you need any money?" And I would humbly answer back, "I'll let you know when we do." To have such a benefactor in our corner was a dream come true.

Peter served on Saint Mary's board during the 1950s and became a lifetime honorary member. In large and small ways, he was always there for us, a leader behind the scenes and a force to be reckoned with who was never afraid of a challenge. In 1998, Peter's commitment and generosity became evident when the hospital opened the Peter M. Wege Institute for Mind, Body and Spirit on its downtown campus. Dedicated to Peter's father and his son, the Wege Institute reflects Peter's pioneering vision for complementary holistic health care and preventive medicine in greater Grand Rapids. The Institute promotes complementary treatments including acupuncture, adult and infant massage, reflexology, natural healing, nutrition, herbs, vitamins, and even music therapy as part of its regime. The institute is the fulfillment of a dream for Peter; it gives Saint Mary's a unique medical niche and a purpose in the community. Throughout his life of generosity and benevolence, Peter still sees the Wege Institute as one of his most favorite projects. It serves as a forerunner of greater things to come for Saint Mary's, for our staff, for the sick and the injured and for friends and family who choose our hospital because they "expect something more."

In 2005 the Richard J. Lacks, Sr. Cancer Center was that "something more." It became an innovative center of excellence in the region known as much for its environmental construction as it was for its pioneering cancer treatments. Planned and built in honor of Peter's friend, Richard J. Lacks, Sr., who died from the disease, the Lacks family wanted to build a major cancer hospital right here in Grand Rapids, at Saint Mary's—an institution that would be innovative and unique, that treated people with cancer not with "usual" medicine but with medicine as "unusual." To accomplish this, the capital campaign needed money. I knew where to go. Fully prepared to make my case, armed with reams of documentation, financial statements, outlines and proposals, I called on Peter. There he sat in his home office behind a massive roll-topped desk knowing full well why I had come to see him. "Peter, you always told me that if I ever needed money, I was to come and ask you," I said. "I need $15 million!" Peter snapped his fingers and said, "Ten!" And that was that.

As the design for the Lacks Cancer Center began to take shape, Peter invited me to tour the new Steelcase Wood Plant in Kentwood, Michigan. Inspired in its construction by Peter's earth-friendly stewardship, the plant had been built using LEED concepts —from its landscaping to its lighting, filtration to dust-collection, storage to heating and cooling, and so much more. It was an enlightening experience which led Saint Mary's to incorporate many Wege-driven environmental technologies into the creation of the Lacks Cancer Center. With its opening in 2005, the Center became the first Leadership in Energy and Environmental Design (LEED) hospital in Michigan and only the second in the United States, thanks in no small part to Peter Wege's environmental fervor, his genius, and his determination.

And then came Saint Mary's Southwest in Byron Center in 2007, followed by another LEED-certified facility in 2008, the American Cancer Society's Hope Lodge at Jefferson Avenue and Cherry Street, with its Peter M. Wege Guest House, named in honor of Peter's father. In 2009 the Hauenstein Neuroscience Center opened on the downtown Saint Mary's campus, a model LEED building that enjoyed major Wege financial support and earth-friendly construction. Today there are more LEED-certified buildings in Grand Rapids than in any other city in America, an urban planning accomplishment that can be traced back to Peter Wege's environmental zeal.

Since I first met him, I have learned that there are few people who live their values like Peter Wege, who believes that we should all invest in something greater than ourselves. He has always taken the mission of Saint Mary's Health Care very seriously including our commitment "to care for the poor and the underserved." It is a Catholic tenant he has modeled and practiced all his life, a core value he learned from his father and mother at an early age that people of faith should embrace in the true spirit of the ministry of Jesus Christ.

Look no further than Grand Rapids' Heartside Health Center to discover Peter's humanity. Here was a celebrated Saint Mary's health center that cared for the city's underserved in unique and compassionate ways. But near the end of 2004 we learned that the old clinic, located on Commerce Street, would soon be displaced by another business, and that we would have to vacate the building. Originally, we had hoped to move the health center to a building on Sheldon Street, but after evaluating the Diocese's future plans and space options, we turned to the northwest corner of Division Avenue and Wealthy Street as the clinic's new location. Ironically, the building just happened to have been Peter's boyhood home.

To quote Ecclesiasticus 6:16, "a faithful friend is the medicine of life." And so Peter surrounds himself with loyal people. His sense of humor is disarming. His infectious smile can light up a room, and his laughter can break the silence. In short, Peter Wege loves and celebrates life with his friends. What a great lesson he has taught us all, that God cares for people through people. Indeed, "living is the art of loving; loving is the art of caring; caring is the art of sharing; and sharing is the art of living," said Booker T. Washington.

For Peter, life without friends is like a day without warmth. For years, Peter has celebrated February 19th, his birthday, in grand style. It is much more than simply a day that comes and goes; it is an event, and Peter is its producer. Year to year, Peter's birthday parties have moved from place to place: the Franciscan Life Process Center in Lowell, the fifth level of the Lacks Cancer Center, and the Grand Rapids Art Museum where he and his entourage celebrated a milestone—Peter's 90th in 2010!

One year the medical staff conferred upon Peter the degree of honorary physician and presented him with his own Saint Mary's Health Care white coat. And since every physician should have the tools of the trade, we gave Peter his own stethoscope complete with a set of directions on how to use the instrument! We raised our glasses and toasted our friend, Peter Wege: "Your vision inspires us to relentlessly pursue excellence; your generosity creates unprecedented possibilities; your spirit encourages and motivates us; your jokes make us smile."

But what do you give to a man who seemingly has everything? Once his friends at Saint Mary's gave him what every angel should have: his own star complete with a companion citation suitable for framing. Now everyone can look to the heavens at night, scope out the constellations and point out "Peter Wege" as precisely as Andromeda or the Big Dipper because, indeed, Peter is a star!

Yes, Peter Wege has touched the lives of his friends and, yes, my life, dramatically. He has taught us to "fear not." He has taught us the value of faith and prayer. He has stirred us to always do the right thing for the community. He has inspired our value of making a difference, that we have only one chance to change the world. And so I am indebted to Peter Wege, Saint Mary's guardian angel.

Finally, sensitive and pure of heart, Peter is truly a Renaissance Man who heard the bells ring and got his wings. He is one of my heroes and a hero to so many others he has touched and to those who have sought to touch him, like the complete stranger who wrote a letter to *The Grand Rapids Press* praising Wege and his contributions to our city. He wrote, "Once there was a Jewish carpenter who never asked for pyramids, palaces or conquests. He died penniless, never had his name adorn a building, yet transformed the world through love toward his fellow humans. I appreciate how Mr. Wege emulates the attitude of that carpenter of long ago. I thank him for making my town and its citizens 'richer' in a quiet way." Amen and amen.

An Inspired Journey

The Lacks Family

"We must become the change we want to see in the world."

-Mahatma Gandhi

The trip to Rome had been months in the making, but the event itself was over in what seemed like an instant. Ravaged by Parkinson's, bent and frail yet so adored and beloved, Pope John Paul II, the venerable Holy Father, sat in his well-worn chair looking up at us with piercing eyes. Sitting before thousands of Christendom's faithful, voice barely audible but with an effortless grace and an elegant lightness, he spoke to us privately in a hoarse whisper; I bent low, kissed his ring and wished him well. Then he blessed the cross that had made the demanding pilgrimage to Rome all the way from Michigan. Two years later, he would die, this astonishing man of God, one of the most influential leaders of the twentieth century. But on this miraculous morning in Saint Peter's Square under a cloudless Italian sky, we belonged to him and he was all ours, if only for a moment. There was such joy in it all; it was transformational, an unforgettable experience that will remain with me forever: the anticipation of this calm October day, the chills that ran through us, the glory of God that took our breath away, the magic of His presence, and the grand family that had inspired the long journey.

In January 2005 we officially opened the Richard J. Lacks, Sr. Cancer Center in downtown Grand Rapids. It was built at the corner of Lafayette Avenue and Cherry Street on the site of Saint Mary's historic McAuley Building. The futuristic $45 million facility was described as a "new kind of specialty hospital." Two years in its construction, it would chart new waters in health care. The center was conceived and designed to approach the treatment of cancer in a whole new way. Displayed on the building's fifth floor, engraved on a decorative glass window facing the Lacks Cancer Center outdoor healing garden is a quote from Mahatma Gandhi, "We must become the change we want to see." That says it all.

Change across Grand Rapids is often slow in coming. That's not a bad thing. But for the anxious and the impatient, change never comes fast enough. Invariably it takes the private sector to move things along, to budge the mighty waters. I believe that God's plan is always at work inspiring and motivating the more public movers and shakers and the quiet philanthropists alike across Grand Rapids' community. Looking out my office window, I see the cross that graces the Cathedral of Saint Andrew's steeple, a testament to the Divine and His mysterious ways. It humbles and inspires me. And so it is with the Lacks Cancer Center. It is a tribute to God's plan and the family that was encouraged to make something happen for the greater good, to "become the change we want to see in the world."

When I arrived at Saint Mary's in the spring of 2000 as its new CEO, my vision for the hospital was to transform the usual into the unusual, to create a brand of targeted care that was truly unique. I wanted to make a profound difference for West Michigan with a focus on three distinct clinical areas that would carve a

niche in our medical community: cancer, neuroscience and orthopedics. People who live in Grand Rapids like choice, and they like
good choices. And so my dream was to make Saint Mary's a dis-
tinctive kind of hospital, a choice with manifest differences from
the competition and the status quo. I gave myself ten years.

Before I arrived the wheels were already in motion to develop a cancer center at Saint Mary's. David Ameen, my immedi-
ate predecessor, proposed engaging several core Catholic supporters of the hospital, including Peter Wege, who might be interested
in raising funds. Initially, hospital administrators dreamed small
and sought only $2 million with which to transform the seventh
floor of the hospital into a cancer center. When medical oncologist
Tom Gribbin, M.D. arrived at Saint Mary's shortly before my time
as CEO, a much larger vision began to evolve.

In the realm of mystery and great and moving faith, God
gives us time and opportunity—golden moments to catch the good
within our grasp. In the late 1990s Richard Lacks, Sr. was stricken
with a rare and unusual soft tissue cancer, one of the rarest forms
of sarcoma in the world. The Lacks family rallied around their pa-
triarch, the man who originally founded, along with his father, J.P.
Lacks, one of the city's most successful privately-owned manufacturing ventures, Lacks Enterprises. The company had grown from
a small Grand Rapids die casting venture into a vast multi-state,
family-owned Midwestern automobile parts supplier with annu-
al sales of more than $300 million. Dick Lacks, Sr., who ran the
enterprise, was a man, like his father, destined for greatness. But
now he was gravely ill.

At that time world-class cancer treatment was unavailable
in Grand Rapids. The form of the disease that ravaged Dick Lacks,
Sr. was an enigma to local oncologists. Concerned for his deterio-

rating health, the family considered various Midwestern hospitals, including the University of Michigan Health System and the Mayo Clinic. They were advised to choose one of the two most highly regarded cancer hospitals in the world, MD Anderson in Houston or Memorial Sloan Kettering in New York City. They settled on MD Anderson. Located on the sprawling University of Texas campus, MD Anderson is a preeminent research and teaching hospital well known for its pioneering cancer care. Unlike Mayo and the University of Michigan that cover the medical waterfront, MD Anderson focuses exclusively on cancer care. But Houston is a long way away. The myriad trips to Texas were exhausting for the Lacks family. "We carted my dad back and forth to Houston for three years," Dick Lacks, Jr. told a newspaper reporter. "It was extremely stressful. But our family was fortunate enough to be able to do that." MD Anderson was an ideal setting. It mirrored Grand Rapids' Midwestern values and culture, and its concerned and sensitive staff were as much care givers as they were miracle workers in the field. It was a good fit. The ailing elder Lacks had said during his treatment in Texas that he wished that anyone stricken with cancer in Grand Rapids should have the good fortune and opportunity to come to MD Anderson to be treated.

Early in his father's fight for life, Dick Lacks, Jr. was approached by David Ameen, Saint Mary's President and CEO, asking him if he would join in the fundraising campaign to build a cancer center in Grand Rapids. To complicate his life, Dick's 94-year-old grandfather, J.P. Lacks, was unexpectedly diagnosed with terminal lung cancer. Now there were two family members who were seriously ill. Combined with the need to run the family business and care for his stricken father and grandfather, Dick told Ameen there was just too much going on in his life to get involved.

Down in Houston, vigilant and constrained, Dick would sit for hours with his ailing father watching and waiting. "We knew he was going to die the last six weeks when we were down there," he said. "The sarcoma had traveled from his foot and metastasized to other parts of his body. It wasn't a good situation." And when J.P. Lacks died in April 1999 in Grand Rapids, it turned a bad situation worse. The frail Lacks, Sr. came home from Houston for the funeral and then returned to Texas to wait out the inevitable with his family at his bedside.

Dick was stoic about his father's deteriorating condition. "I would sit in his hospital room in Houston and say to myself in a kind of prayerful way, 'you know, God, something bad is going to happen here, and I need your help to find something good to come out of this.'" That prayerful plea was repeated many times.

Dick and his family were determined to dig deep and find something positive in their misfortune. "We need to do something," he told his family. "Grand Rapids doesn't have a cancer center." While Dick felt there were good doctors here, cancer care was fragmented. "You have to travel all over the city to be treated. We need a cancer center." Dick remembered his earlier conversation with David Ameen and agreed to talk about helping fund a cancer hospital in Grand Rapids. The time was right to do the right thing. The family agreed and became very much engaged to find a way to honor the legacy of Richard Lacks, Sr. "It was all part of God's plan," said Dick.

Barely three weeks had passed since the family had buried J.P. when Dick Lacks, Sr. passed away in May of 1999. With both deaths coming so close together, the family was devastated. Grieving and saddened, "we were looking for some good to come out of this," said Dick. "My father would have wanted this."

Initially, Dick envisioned a partnership with MD Anderson
—a cancer center in Grand Rapids that would be affiliated with the
hospital in Texas. David Ameen, Dick, and Tom Gribbin, M.D.
flew to Houston and presented their idea. But the Houston hospital
didn't think it would be a good fit. Instead, they encouraged the
Saint Mary's group to pursue their own dream of a cancer center
in Grand Rapids, a vision that would eventually evolve on a grand
scale that would rival even MD Anderson.

Motivated by the loss of his father, Dick was determined
to make a lasting difference. So was the senior Lacks' widow, the
former Jane Morrissey, her daughter, Pat Teets, and Dick's brother,
Kurt. The family approached Saint Mary's with a proposed gift of
$10 million. But there was a caveat: "You need to match our $10
million with $20 million," Dick told Saint Mary's. And Dick had
other demands, among them large patient rooms with lots of natural light, private bathrooms with showers, room service and many
more amenities that he saw as shortcomings at MD Anderson.
Saint Mary's agreed to meet all of Lacks' requests.

The additional money was raised through a vast capital
campaign spearheaded by a group of influential and caring Catholics in the community – Ken and Noreen Hungerford, Mike and
Sue Jandernoa and John and Nancy Kennedy. Together with Dick
and Judy Lacks and the Lacks family, the Cancer Center's destiny
was assured. At the time, the money that was amassed became the
largest legacy gift in the history of the city and certainly for Saint
Mary's. Pledges came from an array of donors large and small,
from hospital associates to seniors on fixed incomes, from modest
givers to affluent foundations, to some of the city's great Catholic entrepreneurs and philanthropists. Collectively the campaign
raised over $45 million.

Dick was particularly grateful for a large gift from Peter Wege. It would be Wege's second gift to the project. "Without his gifts, the Cancer Center would never have happened," said Dick. "I'll never forget it. I never asked him for any money. Peter just came forward and gave it to us. It was incredible!" Together with Dick, Jane Lacks became a catalyst for the project that would honor her husband. Inspired by faith and family, Dick and Jane and the Lacks family led the way, the Catholic way. After all, Saint Mary's Health Care was Grand Rapids' Catholic hospital; and so it was only natural that this generous Catholic family, a family of faith and conviction, chose to support the Cancer Center with their toil, time and treasure. It was a practice and an obligation the family gladly passed on, an outreach Dick, Sr. would have wanted, and J.P., too. Faith mattered. Community mattered. Service mattered. So did pride and accomplishment in giving back.

Tom Gribbin, M.D. and his Saint Mary's team relentlessly pursued a collaborative vision for the new Cancer Center patterned after MD Anderson in Houston. Supported by unprecedented generosity, the five-story 180,000 square-foot facility embraces every aspect of a patient's life and illness. It is truly a unique model of specialty care with multiple services all in one location, including open interaction among collaborating specialists, and the integration of family and friends into the care giving process. "The patient has the disease but the suffering affects the whole family," Gribbin told a reporter. "No marriage in the world is not changed by breast cancer or prostate cancer. And the way loved ones get better is by helping. So we have to invite them in."

When David Ameen suddenly resigned from Saint Mary's in late 1999, the Lacks Cancer Center became one of my first projects as the hospital's new CEO. The torch had been passed.

Now it was my time to serve Saint Mary's and become a part of God's plan, to "be a part of the change we wanted to see in the world."

With the demolition of the McAuley Building came an opportunity that I could not pass up. Atop the aging structure stood an old weathered cross that had been there for over a hundred years. At the time, Robert Rose was Bishop of the Diocese of Grand Rapids. I asked him if he thought the cross could be blessed by the Pope and then installed on top of the Lacks Cancer Center. "Do you think we could have an audience with the Pope if we brought the cross to the Vatican?" I asked.

One thing led to another. Bishop Rose wrote several letters on our behalf. But when the old cross was taken down, we discovered it was in such disrepair from multiple lightning strikes that a new cross would have to be created. And so the wheels were put in motion to fashion a replica of the original McAuley cross.

When Bishop Rose retired in late 2002 he left the challenge of having the cross blessed in Rome to his successor, Bishop Kevin Britt, who had been appointed Bishop for the Diocese of Grand Rapids by Pope John Paul II. Was this another part of God's plan? The high priest of his flock, Bishop Britt was a kind and pious man. He became a good friend to Saint Mary's and to me. "Do you think it's a crazy idea to have the cross blessed by the Pope?" I asked our new Bishop. My friends and Saint Mary's colleagues thought I had lost my mind! But Britt was undaunted by the wild proposal and told me he thought it could be done, and, yes, he could help make it happen. As it turned out, Britt was very well connected. He called his old friend Cardinal Edmund Szoka, the former Archbishop of Detroit, who was serving in Rome as the president of the Governatorate of the Vatican City State, the closest thing the tiny city-state has to a mayor. Cardinal Szoka was also a high ranking and powerful assistant to the Pope. Britt once worked with Szoka in Detroit and he also served at the Vatican for a time. Britt and the Cardinal were fast friends and very familiar with the process required to arrange for a Papal blessing. Britt was fluent in Italian and knew everyone in Rome, including Pope John Paul II. With Szoka's help Britt was optimistic that an audience with the Pope could be arranged.

With Bishop Britt paving the way, a far-reaching trip to Rome for the blessing of the cross began to unfold. It took months to plan. There were times when I didn't think we could pull it off. Fortunately, the Vatican was very cooperative and provided us with enough tickets for the sizable group I hoped to take along for the pilgrimage to Italy. Marlene Landstra, Dick Lacks, Sr.'s sister; her husband, Jerry; and Marlene's three daughters; Father Mark Przybysz; Monsignor Bill Duncan; Lacks Cancer Center architect, Bob Miller and his wife; Saint Mary's COO, Jim Miller and his wife; Marsha Casey from Trinity Health and her mother, Joann; Dick Lacks, Jr.'s sister, Pat Teets; Dick Lacks, Sr.'s widow, Jane; my wife, Gayle; our two sons, Philip and Matthew; Philip's wife, Natalie; and Bishop Britt.

Using a travel agency in Detroit familiar with planning trips to Rome and the Vatican, Bishop Britt, Father Mark, and I meticulously organized the trip down to the last detail. Simultaneously, an exact reproduction of the old ornamental McAuley cross was created, a glistening four-foot high golden Celtic prototype based on the original design. Upon its completion, we carefully packaged and cradled the cross in a reinforced cushioned box and shipped it off to Italy via UPS. Its blessing by the Pope was scheduled for the morning of October 8, 2003.

For our entourage, all roads indeed led to Rome. It was a mystical destination, a monumental imperial city of visible history almost frozen in time, a place of wistful yearnings and grand illusions with its enduring Italian influence.

Our hotel, The Leonardo DaVinci, was the perfect gathering place for our group. Located near the city center, we were within easy walking distance to most of the traditional Roman sites and just a short private bus ride to St. Peter's Basilica. Our mornings were filled with celebration, our days with grand excursions, our nights with anticipation and camaraderie. The old stone walls echoed with history (that Rome was not built in a day); the city's broad porticos and stately columns reflected the hustle-bustle of our Roman holiday; the observations of Dryden from his Imitation of Horace expressed centuries ago rang true: "Happy the man and happy he alone, he who can call today his own." We treasured our time together, especially daily Mass celebrated at various churches in the city, including the Cathedral of Rome, at the gravesite of Saint Peter in the Basilica, and at the North American College led by Bishop Britt and even Cardinal Szoka. It was a first-class trip, a pilgrimage of magical proportions.

The morning of Wednesday, October 8, was cool and calm in legendary Rome. We boarded our bus for the short ride to St. Peter's Square. Even early in the day, tourists were everywhere amidst the hustle-bustle of the Vatican. The Pope was scheduled to appear about 10:00 a.m. with the blessing of our cross planned for 10:30. We soon learned that there are three kinds of time in Vatican City: real time, Roman time and Papal time. We were on Papal time.

The beauty of St. Peter's in all its glory left us breathless and in awe. Jane and I had special tickets allowing us to sit only a few yards from the outdoor chancel that was covered by a large white awning. The rest of our group was seated in chairs to the side of the stage with a perfect view of the Pope, his entourage and the blessing. Around us, seated and standing, were thousands of people who had come to the square to catch a glimpse of John Paul II. There were brides and grooms who had come to have their unions sanctified; priests and cardinals who just wanted to be near their Pontiff; and sundry people from all over the world who had brought various trinkets and assorted items to be blessed by the Holy Father.

Pope John Paul arrived in his "Popemobile" and motored through the massive crowds waving and greeting everyone who looked his way. Eventually, he took his place on the stage surrounded by his assistants, including Bishop Britt and Cardinal Szoka. Seated near the front, Jane and I had been given special instructions about what to say, what not to say, and what protocol to follow once we joined the Pope on the stage. It was all orchestrated and coordinated right down to the minute, it seemed. But the minutes were ever slow in coming.

As our moment neared, Jane whispered to me that she didn't think she could go up to the stage and greet the Pope. I turned to her and said, "Even if I have to carry you in my arms, you're going up there!" As the cross was brought out on to the stage and set before the Pope, I knew the time was near. Transfixed, we were motioned to come forward. Bishop Britt whispered something in the John Paul's ear. Jane and I stood near the cross. We drew closer. Not knowing what to say, I congratulated the Pope on his Jubilee; he smiled a grateful smile. I bent forward and kissed his ring. Nervously, Jane shook his hand but said nothing. Again Bishop Britt leaned down and told Pope John Paul who we were and why we had come so far, "to have our cross blessed." The Pope smiled and spoke in a low hoarse voice. *"Benedico questa croce nel nome del Padre, del Figlio e dello Spirito Santo. Amen"* (I bless this cross in the name of the Father, the Son and the Holy Spirit. Amen). And with that, it was over. But what a glorious opportunity, to see all of our hard work and planning come to fruition.

Back in Grand Rapids, construction of the Lacks Cancer Center had begun. Tom Gribbin, M.D.'s vision for a patient and family-friendly hospital began with the razing of the McAuley Building. It would be replaced by a revolutionary new facility for the entire community, transforming bricks and mortar into compassion, caring and world class medicine. In addition to his monetary gift, Peter Wege donated all of the hospital's Steelcase furniture. LEED-certified, the Lacks building was a structural tour de force, again influenced by Wege's passion for conservation and his fervor for all things environmental. It was truly a "green" enterprise, Michigan's first LEED-certified hospital. From the time a patient and his or her family and friends enter the lobby through the front door, the Lacks experience becomes apparent. Patients and their families no longer have to endure a city-wide obstacle course for their treatment and care traveling from one place to the next, one doctor to the next, one treatment facility to another. Now everything was right there in one centralized location. The Lacks Cancer Center is focused on one thing—the healing of cancer, period.

The Lacks cupola became a familiar structure at the corner of Lafayette Avenue and Cherry Street. At sunset, it stood out like a welcoming beacon against Grand Rapids' cityscape. Only one thing was missing—the cross that had been blessed by the Pope in Rome.

A few months after our journey to Italy, we held a ceremony to dedicate the new cross. It was gently lifted out of its shipping box and carefully raised into position by a large crane. One person present at its official installation said the cross had "an uncanny energy about it, a mystical quality." It was a symbol not unlike the cross on top of the Cathedral of Saint Andrew that I could see from my office window. The cross meant something. And now the Lacks cross meant something too, blessed by Pope John Paul II in far-away Vatican City.

When the Richard J. Lacks, Sr. Cancer Center opened its doors in January 2005, it was a glorious day for Saint Mary's, for Trinity Health and for greater Grand Rapids. The highly anticipated facility was billed as a "new kind of hospital, a healing environment where compassion is built into its design and care regime." In time it would attract skilled oncologists and staff from across the country and around the world.

Sadly, Bishop Kevin Britt was not among the attendees at the Center's grand opening. The victim of a rare brain disorder, he died suddenly on May 15, 2004 (see the chapter, "The People's Bishop"). Today, when I pass by the Cancer Center or see its cross, blessed by the Pope and gleaming in the sunlight, I think of Jesus and then I think of Bishop Britt and mourn his passing. He would have relished the day when the Lacks cross was officially lifted into place.

Not enough can be said about the family whose name the Cancer Center bears, about the man it honors, about all of the donors who contributed large and small, about the doctors and staff, and the designers and builders of this wonderful place. It will endure and endure. For Dr. Tom Gribbin, this was his dream come true.

When Richard Lacks, Sr. died in May 1999, it was not the end but a beginning. His death was a foreshadowing of life, of things to come. "No question about it, this Center has fulfilled everything we thought it would for the community," said Dick Lacks, Jr. "Since the Cancer Center has been built, the experiences that people have had are a testament to its success. All you ever hear is, 'It's first class!' That's very gratifying. And to me that's all that matters at the end of the day. It's just wonderful."

And so it is – The Richard J. Lacks, Sr. Cancer Center – a vision, a dream and a testament to one family's inspired journey "to become the change we want to see in the world."

A Righteous Man

Ken Hungerford

"A satisfied customer is the best business strategy of all."

-Michael LeBoeuf

Ask his close friends to describe Ken Hungerford and you will find consensus on strategy, wine and the University of Notre Dame. "The essence of strategic planning," said the Harvard Business School's Michael Porter, "is choosing what not to do. It is about making choices and trade-offs and deliberately choosing to be different." With that, Ken Hungerford would agree. And as a collector of fine wine, he has no equal. After all, wrote Robert Louis Stevenson, "wine is like bottled poetry." Among other things, that would make Ken Hungerford a poet.

When it comes to his alma mater, that's another story. Around South Bend where faith and football are practically synonymous, you won't find a more loyal cheerleader than Ken Hungerford, especially on the gridiron. "While other universities have histories," wrote Fred Shapiro, editor of *The Yale Book of Quotations*, "Notre Dame has legends!" Every autumn, Catholic Notre Dame is known far and wide for winning, and sometimes for losing. But it matters not. Said former football coach, Lou Holtz, "I don't think God cares who wins, but His mother does!"

Together with strategy, wine and Notre Dame, I would add this description in praise of Ken Hungerford: an all-around good guy. His history is worth reading. His exemplary life story is worth a second look. We can all learn from it and from him. Moreover, Ken Hungerford is a gentleman, a gentle man with the heart of an angel; he is his father's son, someone who puts more into the world than he takes out, whom the Old Testament calls a Tzaddik, a "righteous man." Without Ken Hungerford, Saint Mary's Health Care would be a lesser institution. All of us would be smaller people in the larger scope of life. Ken Hungerford sets the bar, and we try to measure up.

Dark and dawning, December 31, 1973 began like any other day. The sun came up right on schedule like a sacred mystery; the frosty sky hung quietly over northern Michigan. Fresh snow had fallen during the night and covered the frozen landscape. But this near perfect New Year's Eve day would end far differently than anybody imagined.

It was cloudy and cold, only five degrees by 6:00 a.m. The temperature would climb to a mere 18 degrees by mid-afternoon; there was a gentle wind but mostly there was only silence with an ominous chill in the air. Across the nation, the Watergate investigation was heating up. President Nixon was ranting and reeling, and gas rationing was the order of the day. There were long lines at America's service stations. Anxious drivers were befuddled, questioning why oil had risen to $10 a barrel with no end in sight.

Ken Hungerford's father, at 52, was a giant in the city's business community. He was a senior member of the accounting firm, K.G. Hungerford & Co., and he was president of Edge Saw Manufacturing, a successful company that produced cutting and processing equipment for the foam rubber industry. He was one of the most respected businessmen in West Michigan.

Despite the perception that all was not right with the world, the senior Hungerford was determined to end the year on a high note and begin 1974 with new hope and optimism. Life was good. A holiday skiing trip had gone well in northern Michigan, but now it was time to drive south, home to Grand Rapids to ring in the New Year.

Cheerful and carefree, driving south on Michigan Highway 115, seven miles north of Cadillac, Hungerford's car momentarily crossed the center line and collided violently, head-on, with a car heading north. "It was a horrific accident," said family friend and attorney, Jim Brady. "Ken, Sr. was killed. It was a significant event."

Suddenly, the air was full of poignant farewells and heartbreaking goodbyes. The elder Ken Hungerford was dead. He was here, and then he was gone, simply flown away. Now he was with God just as God had been with him in life. His wife, Sally, was in serious condition. Their young daughter, Susan, was treated at a local hospital. The driver of the other car, Jane Booth and her passenger, Edwin Booth, both of Detroit, were injured but alive.

Planning his father's funeral, young Ken Hungerford felt despair pass over him like a cold wind taking him to a place he had never been before. "Every moment dies a man," said Tennyson, "and every moment one is born." And so, with his father's death, Ken Hungerford was suddenly thrust into a new beginning. He was only 27. "It was a life-changing event in his life," said Ken's brother-in-law, John Byington. "He had to step in and take over the family business. He was just kind of thrown into this."

Despite his unanticipated role, the loss of his father would stay with Ken Hungerford all his life. Rarely a day goes by that he does not think about him. The same inner voice he heard as a child he would hear as an adult – "what will we do without you?"

Ken Hungerford grew up in a mostly carefree time and place. As a youth, he lived in the Garfield Park area of Grand Rapids and later moved to a neighborhood near Breton Village. "They were a very distinguished, large Catholic family," said Jim Brady. "We lived in the same general neighborhood. Ken and I went to Catholic Central High School together. I was from Saint Francis Parish."

But Ken's youth was not without its misfortune. When he was very young, his mother died. "I don't know if he ever really knew her," said Brady. Ken's father re-married; Sally Hungerford became a loving stepmother. "She was a very sweet lady," said Brady.

At Notre Dame, Ken studied finance and business and earned his degree in accounting. While Brady knew Ken casually at Catholic Central, "I really got to know him when I was a third year law student at Notre Dame. I kind of mentored him." Ken studied law for a year but dropped out and taught school at one of Grand Rapids Catholic academies.

Talk with Ken about his formative years and invariably, Big Whitefish Lake will enter the conversation. Located 40 miles north of Grand Rapids just west of Pierson, the cottage the family bought in 1965 was as much a getaway as a hideaway. It was a refuge, a sanctuary, an oasis, an emotional piece of property where the Hungerford family could escape and take delight in the world.

Big Whitefish Lake was a safe and tranquil place with its long wooded shoreline, clear hills and natural wildlife. Ironically, the cottage next door was owned by the Byington family. Ken was attracted as much to the Byington's daughter, Noreen, as he was to the pristine lake, majestic sunsets and the surrounding pine forest.

"I knew her in high school," said Ken. "We were the same age." So during his cottage years, Ken and Noreen rekindled their friendship from Catholic Central. The large gazebo near the curve of the lake shore became a kind of courting territory. Ken was smitten; so was Noreen. They were married in 1968. So for years and years, Big Whitefish Lake became an attraction like no other and a long memory. "Growing up there was magical," said John Byington. "It was a real bonding thing. Our families were very centered. The Hungerford and Byington kids still gather there."

After college, Ken joined his father's CPA firm. Everyone called him "Kenny." He learned the business under his father's tutelage. "Hungerford, Sr. was anything but a 'bean-counter,'" said Brady. "He was a wheeler-dealer in the best sense of the word. He was sharp; he was good looking, articulate and very tough. You didn't want to be across the table from him. They worked hard and they played hard, and they were very good businessmen."

Working with his father, Ken learned all the right things, all the good things. "But he didn't have his father's hard outer crust," Brady said.

Ken's father was very close to Richard Lacks, Sr., who had made a small investment in a start-up automotive parts manufacturer and supplier called ADAC. The two families – the Hungerfords and the Lacks – were very close.

"He was very good friends with my father-in-law, Richard Lacks, Sr.," said Jim Teets. "They were different in age, but I think

Dick really admired Ken for his professionalism, because he was a CPA." Over the years, the Hungerfords had provided the Lacks family with a lot of tax help and business advice with their company, Lacks Enterprises.

When his father was killed in the car accident on New Year's Eve Day, 1973, Ken was understandably devastated. Life was never quite the same again. Ken picked up the pieces of the family business and simply moved on.

"Accounting was our family's business," Ken said. "And I did like it." Eventually, Ken had the opportunity to leave the family CPA firm and join Lacks Enterprises when they bought controlling interest in ADAC.

But there was a problem. "Who are we going to get to run this company?" they asked. They wanted a professional manager, someone they could trust. "And I think the first person they thought of was Ken," said Teets. "Dick, Sr. didn't think Ken would do it. And Kenny said 'When do I start?!'"

Under Ken's leadership, the enterprise grew and prospered. "He helped grow this company," said Teets, who started working for ADAC in 1993. "Ken got here in 1986. He was the guy most responsible for getting us from $25 million to over $100 million. Today, we're just shy of $200 million!"

When Teets came to ADAC from the insurance business, Ken was his direct boss. "Ken was president and CEO. My father-in-law was chairman. I didn't know anything about cars. So Ken really mentored me."

Ken Hungerford was a businessman through and through. "I would say he's a CPA in a sales and marketing body," said Teets. "My father-in-law really thought the world of Ken and Noreen."

Teets figures Ken's talent for business and accounting was in his DNA. "It probably came from his father and some of it came from Catholic Central and Notre Dame. After his dad died in the car accident, all of a sudden Ken was kind of thrust into certain situations as a young man. And it's all about survival. He had to do this. And I think he discovered he was pretty good at it. It was fun."

Ken may have been good with numbers, but his true talent was that of a visionary – someone who could see the future. "As a planner and a strategic thinker, Ken got all that from his father," said Jim Brady.

"When you start to really dive deep with Ken," said Teets, "whether it's fund raising or leading a capital campaign, he'll come up with the theoretical, and the next thing you know, you have a real live plan. He can do that! He'll get up there with his white boards and markers, and he'll start drawing the vision, doing all the head stuff. He'll say 'here's where I'm going.' He'll have all of these flow charts and sometimes, he'll drive you crazy, but at least you get the vision and the concept, and sometimes, the solution."

With the senior Lacks demise, the family was determined to establish a cancer center in Grand Rapids patterned after MD Anderson in Houston where Lacks was being treated; (see the chapter, "An Inspired Journey" to learn more about the Lacks Cancer Center). "Much of the philosophy and even the design of our Center was based on what the Lacks family experienced down in Texas," Ken said. MD Anderson was one of the premier cancer centers in the United States, and the Lacks family wanted a facility just like it right here in our community.

"In the Catholic faith, May 13, 1999 was Ascension Thursday. It was almost like Dick willed himself to die on that day," said Teets. "We all went to the hospital in Houston to say our goodbyes; then we went to Mass as a family, and arranged to have his body flown back to Grand Rapids."

The campaign to raise money for the Richard J. Lacks, Sr. Cancer Center at Saint Mary's needed effective leadership. The campaign was far-reaching and aggressive across the Catholic community. "There were three couples who co-chaired the campaign," said Teets. "Ken and Noreen Hungerford, Mike and Sue Jandernoa, and John and Nancy Kennedy. Gosh, you talk about the perfect trifecta of couples! They were all connected with raising money for Grand Rapids' Catholic schools." Over time, the capital campaign raised over $45 million for the Lacks Cancer Center, an unprecedented amount of money in Grand Rapids.

"I was blessed with good parents and a good education and certainly a Catholic-Christian upbringing," said Ken. "So I had the values of someone who went to private Catholic schools. Those values stay with you. Mike and Sue Jandernoa, Dick and Judy Lacks, and John and Nancy Kennedy have been instrumental. They are very generous people and, in most cases, their involvement is very quiet. And that's one of the strengths of Grand Rapids."

And the campaign's success was based on a solid strategic plan, thanks to Ken Hungerford's vision for the project. "Everything Saint Mary's has done subsequent to that has been accomplished because a planning process was followed with a stated mission, a stated vision, some operating principles and the execution of a long-term plan," Ken said. Ken, who was a member of Saint Mary's Board of Trustees, brought a new level of strategic insight to the hospital and its long-range strategy.

Eventually Ken's talent as a planner caught the eye of Saint Mary's Health Care. Ken and Noreen were strong Catholics, so an association with Saint Mary's made sense. Having Ken and

Noreen co-chair the Cancer Center campaign was a real plus. Like Ken, I have a real passion for planning, so in 2002, we asked him if he would chair Saint Mary's Planning Committee. I could not have asked for a better person to complement my desire to keep the hospital focused.

"Planning is more than just sitting around thinking about stuff," said Ken. "It involves gathering data. I've always been quite healthy. I've never been in a hospital. But I have a good understanding of Saint Mary's. We're very active practicing Catholics so I have a real affinity toward Saint Mary's."

Ken and I have a long history together. "Phil and I lived in the same Forest Hills area," said Ken. "We both had children who went to the same grade schools and high schools." At the time, I was still at Butterworth Hospital.

"Ken has always been great for the hospital for advice and counsel," said Brady. But as good as Ken was at envisioning and strategic planning, he had a secret weapon, his wife, Noreen.

"Ken's wife would say 'he's the same guy I married,'" said Teets. "They're kind of a yin and yang. They each have their strengths. Ken is really the more reserved. Noreen is more full of energy."

John Byington, Noreen's brother, agrees. "Language is one of her strong suits, a real strength," he said. "She wanted to be an interpreter. So she can express herself in English. She can go head-to-head with tough personalities. She's smart and tough. Noreen and Ken make a great couple."

Jim Brady agrees. "When you're around Noreen, you can't keep your composure without laughing. She and Ken are very funny people. They are just delightful!"

No profile about Ken Hungerford is complete without a mention of his wine collection. "He has between 4,000 and 5,000 bottles of wine down in his basement," said Teets.

"Yes, he has quite a wine cellar at his home," Byington said. "Once Noreen wanted to expand their kitchen and thought it would be a tough sell to convince Ken. But he was more than agreeable. As it turned out, his wine cellar was right underneath the kitchen. Expand the kitchen and you expand the wine cellar! That's strategic thinking!" But strategy without tactics is like day without night. Perhaps legendary British actor, comedian and BBC radio personality, Frank Muir, said it best: "Strategy is buying a bottle of fine wine when you take a lady out for dinner. Tactics is getting her to drink it."

If wine is the drink of the gods, then Ken Hungerford is a godly man. "I think you can probably make a good analogy between a maturing bottle of wine and a successful business," said Teets. "Open no bottle before its time; don't launch a business before its time. Today, at his age and maturity and through the experiences he's had, he really knows when it's the right time to pull the cork on that nice bottle of Merlot."

Like a business, or any organization, a bottle of wine is a living, breathing thing. And so it is with Saint Mary's Health Care —like old wine it continues to improve with age.

And Teets loves to tell people his favorite Ken Hungerford wine story. "At our wedding in 1983 at Cascade Hills Country Club, my father-in-law made the mistake of letting his friends order whatever they wanted to drink. Some people ordered bottles of wine. Ken, being the wine connoisseur, ordered a bottle and there was a new waiter who didn't know quite how to use a corkscrew. Ken offered to show the young waiter how it is done. So he pulled the cork out and the metal part of the cork screw nailed the poor kid in the head and I think knocked him out momentarily. Ken just felt terrible! So the next day Ken went to the Cascade Hills Country Club for Sunday brunch and who's there but this poor waiter with a big shiner," said Teets. So "here's to the corkscrew," said W.E.P. French, "a useful key to unlock the storehouse of wit, the treasury of laughter, the front door of fellowship, and the gate of pleasant folly." But take it from Ken Hungerford—do use it wisely (and carefully)!

When Ken Hungerford's father died in that tragic car accident in 1973, it must have felt like the end of the world. But Ken prevailed. So did his character. It matured. So did his integrity. It grew in stature. He would never forget the man who gave him so much—his father, who was his light of the world.

When one of his half-brothers took his own life, Ken recoiled. Death was no stranger to the Hungerford family.

In 2010 misfortune struck the family once again, when Ken's younger brother, Rick, died of leukemia. Life seemed very tentative. But life went on.

"Anyone who has never known ill-fortune has never known himself or his own virtue," said Irish scientist, Robert Mallet. And so Ken Hungerford became very familiar with his own reflection in the mirror. He saw himself, while others saw the face of an angel.

Above all, Ken is not a small person. "Little minds are tamed and subdued by misfortune, but great minds rise above it," wrote Washington Irving. Indeed, Ken has risen above life's ill fortunes.

Through it all, Ken Hungerford has never stopped his giving ways. In his goodness, he has always given much more than he has taken. It is a sign of his godliness. How fortunate we all are. He is blessed; and we are all blessed to know such a righteous man.

The Altar Boy

John C. Canepa

"Success unshared is failure."
-John Canepa

L ooking west out his fourth floor office window on Campau Avenue, octogenarian John Canepa has a perfect view of Grand Rapids' westward cityscape. Impeccably dressed in a cuff-linked light blue shirt, conservative tie, suspenders and navy blue pin-striped suit, Canepa proudly surveys the city he might have imagined when he first came to town over 40 years ago. Below, the Grand River ambles slowly southward. Across the river, the stately Van Andel Public Museum stands proudly as does the downtown campus of Grand Valley State University. To the northwest, Canepa can see the Gerald R. Ford Presidential Museum with its expansive front lawn stretching along the meandering Grand River. Out of view to the south and east stands Grand Rapids' popular Van Andel Arena; to the northeast, the immense DeVos Place Convention Center; and up along Michigan Street Hill, a vast medical complex has blossomed. Six blocks to the south and to the east, Saint Mary's Health Care, the city's venerable Catholic hospital, serves a dedicated constituency nurturing the underserved and the general public alike. For four decades and counting, with watchful eyes and consummate wisdom, John Canepa has looked after our hospital with a keen civic vision to ensure its rightful place in the community. Indeed, he is one of our most revered angels. Saint Mary's owes him so much. "Success unshared is failure," he has always said. With his intelligence, good judgment and counsel, Saint Mary's could not fail.

John Canepa was born on August 26, 1930. It was stifling in provincial Newburyport, Massachusetts. It had been an insufferably hot month with 21 straight days of temperatures over 100 degrees. Located 36 miles northeast of Boston, Newburyport was a close-knit sleepy coastal town of 10,000. It has since grown to twice that size but remains a historic seaport with a homey village feel. In 2005, it was chosen The Most Beautiful City in America (for communities with a population between 15,000 and 20,000).

Over eighty years ago Newburyport was quiet and quaint and distinctly old-world. The smell of brine from the Atlantic Ocean saturated the heavy air. Federal-style houses dotted the Italian, Polish and Greek districts where immigrant neighborhoods banded together in ethnic enclaves to preserve their deep-rooted cultures. The scent of freshly caught fish baking in the oppressive noon-day heat wafted up from the wharves along Water Street. Deliveries of coal and molasses arrived by barge. Lumber yards fed the shipbuilding trade, and the imposing Ruth Shoe Company looked down on Market Square. Here, anybody's business was everybody's business. Newburyport also had many claims to fame among them, being the home of President John Quincy Adams, for a time.

This was also the hometown of John C. Canepa—a straight shooter who grew up on the East Coast but grew old in Grand Rapids. When he was born on that hot day in August, it was no ordinary time across Massachusetts. Herbert Hoover was president and these were the Depression years. The American way of life had been shaken to its foundation. The country was clinically depressed. "Americans were flat on their backs," wrote journalist Jonathan Alter. "They began to think that this convulsive change in their lives was permanent. Suicide rates tripled. Sixteen million people found themselves without jobs, many with three or more dependents." When Franklin Roosevelt celebrated his first Inauguration in March of 1933, 10,000 American banks had failed.

Despite the hard times, Canepa recalls growing up simply and innocently in Newburyport; he was a good Catholic boy who was exposed to a churchly upbringing. The family went to Mass every Sunday where they prayed and lighted candles asking God to end the misery that plagued America. Canepa marched in church parades and acted in religious pageants. He was an altar boy with a calm, collected exterior yet with a weighty intensity on the inside. At Immaculate Conception Catholic School, the nuns taught him well. "Sister Antonina was my first grade teacher," said Canepa. "Sister Bernadette was my second grade teacher. They made a lasting impression on me: to have respect for other people and share things with others."

The Canepas were a poor Italian family. The Depression years had hit Massachusetts and Newburyport hard. This was hardly a dust bowl town, but nonetheless, its citizens suffered from worrisome unemployment and empty stomachs. It was not uncommon to hear a knock on the door with the proverbial "Brother, can you spare a dime?" or encounter bread lines of men with scruffy beards and tattered suits grateful for a hot meal. But Newburyport took care of its own. Those who had jobs were fortunate. Mayor Bossy Gillis complained of sweat shops where men worked eight hour days six days a week for $2.50 a day.

Everybody was broke, but life in Newburyport went on despite the hard times.

"My father was a truck driver," said Canepa. "Every morning he would drive into Boston and pick up a load of fruit and vegetables and make his deliveries all day to restaurants and grocery stores. I often went along for the ride. My mother was a homemaker and took care of my younger brother and sister and me. We only had heat in the kitchen. In the cold of winter, each of us kids had a rock that we put in the oven. We wrapped the rocks in towels and took them to bed with us so our feet would stay warm at night," Canepa recalls.

In the face of strife and privation, people found time and energy for social activities. There were dances run by the St. Paul's Men's Association, all-star wrestling at City Hall, performances by Irish minstrels at the Immaculate Conception Parish, and Depression dances that were held at the Plum Island Pavilion. "We were never unhappy," wrote resident historian, Ralph Ayers, who knew the Canepa family. "If someone had half a loaf of bread more than someone else, they would share it with the ones who didn't have any. And that, I think, was a good experience to go through."

During his formative years in Newburyport and growing up on Merrimac Street, Canepa's memory of the Depression years is vague. He was motivated by perfection and a drive to keep the world in some kind of order despite the chaos. He sought a predictable life. His friends looked up to him, admiring his highly analytical mind. When he was thirteen he worked at his uncle's soda fountain earning $1.25 a week where he learned the value of a day's pay for a day's labor.

At Newburyport High School Canepa stood out. They
called him "Johnny." The 1947 yearbook described him as "a
truly loyal friend, a genial companion, and a fine athlete." Writer
and retired teacher, Jean Wade, now Jean Doyle, inscribed Canepa's yearbook with "To a swell football player." But Canepa
loved baseball best. At Harvard, (1949-1953) he was a standout
second baseman. After college, he played in the semi-professional
league for the Lynn, Massachusetts Red Sox. "One day the manager called me in and said, 'John, you've got a great pair of hands,
and you love the game,' which was his way of telling me I couldn't
hit worth a damn! He advised me to move on." So in 1953 Canepa enlisted in the Navy, the same year he married Marie Olney of
Newburyport.

His experience at sea during the Korean War would serve
him well throughout his life. He learned the value of teamwork and
how everyone plays his part to achieve a goal by working together. For Canepa working on a ship was like running a successful
company with guiding principles, a mission and vision, and pride
in accomplishment. "I think it helped form our personalities," said
Canepa's long-time Grand Rapids friend and fellow Navy man,
David Frey. "It helped form our sense of self. It helped form our
sense of country, a sense of allegiance and purpose."

Canepa began his career in finance in 1958 after a friend
encouraged him to apply for a position at Chase Manhattan Bank.
That same year he enrolled in an MBA program at New York
University Stern School of Business and received his degree in
1960. After five years at Chase, he and Marie moved to Cincinnati
where Canepa became Provident Bank's senior loan officer. Then
in 1970 he was recruited by Old Kent Bank in Grand Rapids. "As
a banker I had always heard about Old Kent, and so I came up to
Grand Rapids for an interview and was impressed with the city,"

Canepa said. "Back then it was a sleepy Midwest town." Eventually he became president of the bank and in 1988 was promoted to Old Kent's Chairman and CEO; he formally retired in 1995. Later he became a consulting principal at Crowe Chizek in Grand Rapids.

Canepa's first encounter with Saint Mary's came in the mid-1970s when he was asked to join the hospital's Board of Trustees. "I'll always remember my first Board meeting," he said. "When the meeting was over, one of the nuns wheeled out a cart with bottles of bourbon, vodka, and scotch and served drinks to the Board members. That was a surprise."

"When I came to Grand Rapids, one of the first things I noticed was that there were hardly any bars downtown," he said in his recognizable Boston brogue. "In Cincinnati where I lived, we'd go out for a drink on our way home from work. Here there was only one restaurant with a bar in the old Pantlind Hotel. Well, times have really changed. After the Van Andel Arena was built, there were 17 restaurants."

Having grown up Catholic, Canepa was drawn to Saint Mary's. He chaired the Board of Trustees for six years and eventually stepped down in the early 1980s. "The challenges then were financial," he recalls. "It was different. Saint Mary's has always been, in my mind, willing to take care of people who couldn't afford a hospital. That's always been part of Saint Mary's culture. So the hospital was always faced with meeting its budget. But the medical profession is still a business; you still have a budget and a balance sheet and income statements. You still have to ask the tough questions: can we afford to do this? How can we raise money? How do we control expenses? That's particularly true as the health and medical care fields have changed. It changed dramatically.

While he was on the Board of Trustees, Canepa developed many relationships in the community and also with the hospital's staff and physicians. "Nowadays, you go into a hospital emergency room, and you're bleeding like hell, and before they'll even look at you, they ask to see your insurance card," said Canepa. "Saint Mary's is different. It has a different culture. It's a different quality of care. I don't know where that attitude comes from other than it's been there for so long. Maybe it's the religious perspective. In most places, the culture is developed from the top down. At Saint Mary's it comes from the bottom up. It's the people who develop the culture. Medicine and technology have changed, but the people haven't changed at all. To me, that's the important thing."

And he should know. "Believe me, I've been a patient at Saint Mary's enough times to appreciate this. I've had six surgeries – an ulcer, prostate, three hernia operations and one back surgery. It's a great place," he said. "That difference is apparent when you walk through the front door. It's how you're treated, just the friendly atmosphere when you walk in. It's a glad-to-see-you-type of place! When you go to Saint Mary's, you're a person, not a number. The focus is on the patient, not always on the bottom line."

When it comes to Saint Mary's, Canepa is an entertaining storyteller. "I had to have a hernia operation," he recalls. "So I drove to the hospital and parked my car in the lot and had the outpatient surgery in the morning. After the operation a nurse came in and asked if someone was picking me up? I said yes, my son is meeting me. So they brought me down in a wheelchair and pushed me out the front door. I said, 'You can just leave me here. My son's picking me up.' So the nurse left. And I got up and walked to my car and drove away and went back to work. That's a true story!" he said laughingly.

Before I came to Saint Mary's in the spring of 2000, I hadn't had many dealings with John. I had only met him casually. But I soon came to realize what an important role he had played at Saint Mary's and what an asset he was. Because of his position at Old Kent Bank, John was an indispensable part of the hospital's history. I think the world of him. Little did I know that when I came to the hospital as its new CEO that John would become such a wonderful resource not only for me but for everyone at Saint Mary's. Successful leaders have a high degree of integrity. They really do what is best for the organization rather than what is best for themselves. That has always been John's key to his success. And so I learned from him. Everyone at the hospital learned from him.

John and I quickly developed a close relationship. Every time I turned around John was the one person I could talk to. He knew the history of Saint Mary's. He's been a great coach for me. He's an angel! Best of all, John knows where all the land mines are located around Saint Mary's and in Grand Rapids. He will always tell you about the good side of people, their strengths and their contributions. We have similar outlooks on life.

"Whenever Phil and I meet, we warmly greet each other," said Canepa. "It's become a custom. Phil's a great guy!"

And John's a great guy, and he's a wonderful Catholic! He's a servant-leader. As a former Board member, he's part of Saint Mary's Emeritus Board, which he started. The Emeritus Board gets together once a quarter for lunch. I attend these luncheons and bring everyone up to date on hospital developments.

John's impact on Grand Rapids' future and economic growth has been substantial. He was once described as "a banker by trade and a community servant by heart." As a member of the Downtown Development Authority, he led efforts to bring major cultural and business organizations to the city. With Dick DeVos and David Frey, he is a leader of Grand Action, a non-profit organization that identifies and supports downtown building and revitalization projects, like the Van Andel Arena, DeVos Place Convention Center, the Civic Theater, and the Michigan State University College of Human Medicine. John was also an active supporter of the new Grand Rapids Art Museum, and he served on the boards of the Grand Rapids Symphony, the Grand Valley State University Foundation, Grand Valley State University Seidman College of Business, Aquinas College, Sacred Heart Seminary, Interlochen Center for the Arts, and John Cabot University in Rome.

Still, Canepa always had time for Saint Mary's. He continues to look out for the hospital to ensure that it plays a high-profile role in the community, and that Saint Mary's always has a seat at the table. His counsel was particularly important during the development of the Van Andel Institute and eventually, in the development of the Michigan State University College of Human Medicine in Grand Rapids. He wanted Saint Mary's to be a community stakeholder and be in the game.

"The key to the development of MSU's medical school," said Canepa, "was that it be a collaborative effort with all the hospitals and with Grand Valley State University. One of the challenges for the location of the medical school was geography. Should it be located on the Medical Mile or closer to Saint Mary's?"

John lives by his motto: "Success unshared is failure." Throughout his banking career, John wanted to share his civic vision, his experience and his success. He was analytical.

He was observant. He was helpful and reliable, and he was precise. John is also calm, cool and collected. In this business, that's a real plus, combined with his capacity to be patient and understanding.

Canepa's fundraising activities for Saint Mary's have been instrumental to our growth. "I think the important thing is to develop a structure to raise money," he said. "If you want to raise a dollar, 80 cents will come from 20 per cent of the people. No question that the 80/20 Rule applies. People in the community have a respect for Saint Mary's Hospital. Generosity is part of the Catholic culture."

Both the Catholic Church and John Canepa have come a long way since his youth growing up in provincial Newburyport in the 1930s and '40s. Jokingly, he recalls the sisters at Immaculate Conception Catholic School.

"I survived. I still have the scars!" he said playfully. "I'd go up to the front of the room and the ruler would come out!" Indeed, times have changed and so has the Catholic Church. "I remember going over to Farmington Hills to the Sisters of Mercy when I was on the finance committee. And they had a kind of social function, and I walked into this room and found the sisters were no longer wearing their habits."

Canepa did not and could not achieve success in life without Marie, his wife since 1953. She is practical, hard-working and generous, yet remains intentionally in the background where she provides the foundation for her husband's career. "Marie has been my best friend all those years," said Canepa. "She's been a counselor to me. We met while I was going to prep school outside of Boston. I think we met at a dance."

For John and Marie, Grand Rapids is home. "We both always thought that when I retired from the bank, we'd go back to the Boston area where we had some family, but as it got closer, we both agreed that we'd never leave Grand Rapids for the rest of our lives. We both just love the quality of life here," he said. "We love the people and this place."

And that includes Saint Mary's Health Care. "Success unshared is failure." It's the perfect philosophy that guides a great achiever and a good friend–John Canepa, the Altar Boy from New-buryport.

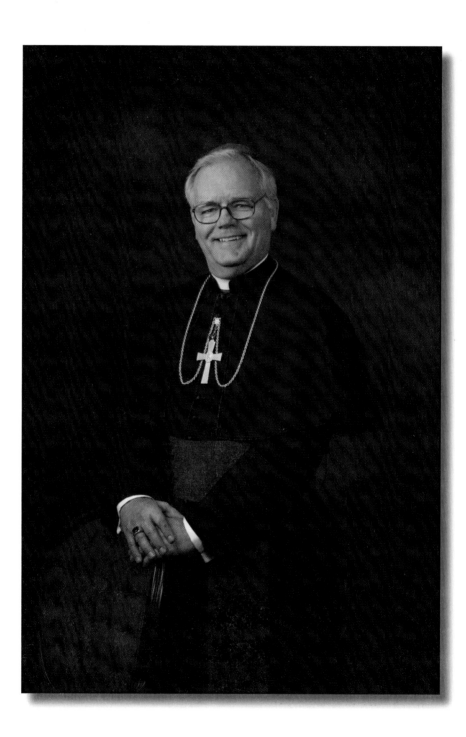

The People's Bishop

Kevin M. Britt
1944 – 2004

*"A pebble cast into a pond causes ripples that spread in all directions.
Each one of our thoughts, words and deeds is like that."*
-Dorothy Day

O nly in his dreams did Kevin Britt imagine that he would
ascend the Catholic Church hierarchy to become a bishop. After all, from age seven he aspired only to be a
priest. That would be enough. In his Detroit home, young Britt
would set up a table as an altar. He used a cardboard box as a
tabernacle. He fashioned a peanut butter jar into a chalice and
Wonder Bread into hosts. His mother gave him a white sheet that
he wore as a vestment. "I had my own little church in the basement," he said. "My mom used to laugh. She'd be upstairs making dinner, and I'd be down there preaching up a storm!" Later in
high school he decided that a religious life would be the life for
him. He pondered and he prayed and waited for an answer. "I'm
convinced that God calls us," he said. "He opens the door and
you walk through it." And so Kevin Britt walked through the door.
Uncommon and exceptional, Britt was a treasure; he was one of
a kind. He cherished people and his community where he was a
model of kindness, mercy and love. He often worked with youth,
nurturing them to espouse a spiritual life. He once asked a group
of high school students to pair off and face each other and look
into each other's eyes. Then he told them, "That's what God looks
like." His unforeseen death in the spring of 2004 was a tragedy; it

was heartbreaking and beyond belief. A great sadness descended upon the Diocese of Grand Rapids. Hardly a day goes by that I do not mourn his passing. He was my mentor, my friend and he was our brother. He was a blessing to us all. As the psalmist wrote, "His life ended like a great sigh." He was suddenly gone and, like an angel, he flew away.

When fall comes to West Michigan, that auburn season of perfection, it is a time of melancholy for some and simply a spectacular season for others. Change is like that. In the cold crisp air that surrounds Resurrection Cemetery, the leaves fall and blow about covering the ground like a colorful shawl. We grieve and learn from the loss. The days grow shorter, the sun sets sooner and rises later. Peaceful and serene, the silence is broken only by the distant drone of traffic along U.S. 131. Not far off, two partially deflated helium balloons mark the graves of deceased relatives. They are gone but not forgotten.

In the cemetery's interior, a massive circular monument with seven great white columns is unmistakable and difficult to miss. It stands proudly and stately straddled by two giant elms that shed their withering leaves in autumn. They fall slowly to the ground covering the gravesites in a carpet of brilliant pur-plish-brown. It is a sign that Michigan's long gray winter is not far off.

At Resurrection Cemetery, there are prominent grave markers nearly hidden by the fallen foliage. There you'll find a grouping of perfectly aligned brass name plates laid into the ground in reverence to the great bishops of the Diocese of Grand Rapids: Henry J. Richter; Michael J. Gallagher (buried in Detroit); Joseph G. Pinten (buried in Marquette); Joseph C. Plagens; Francis J. Haas; Allan J. Babcock; Joseph M. Breitenbeck, and the most recent grave marker, the tenth Bishop of the Diocese of Grand Rapids – Kevin M. Britt.

In the spring of 2004, winter had finally ended and a new season had arrived. Violets and May flowers bloomed, birds sang, and the fragrance of newness and renewal filled the soft air. It was a familiar scene across the region. Life was repeating itself. But this season was different. Only seven months had passed since Kevin Britt had been installed as our spiritual leader succeeding the Most Reverend Robert J. Rose, who had retired. We called Kevin "the people's bishop." That was his calling.

"He loved to be around people," said Father Mark Przybysz at St. Anthony of Padua Church. "He touched a lot of people while he was here." Kevin Britt was that kind of man—godly, gregarious and funny. He loved his community and his flock. He made us laugh and he laughed with us. The air was always full of his playfulness and his Irish wit.

The week of May 9th Bishop Bitt was not feeling well. Earlier in the month he had been in Rome on church business with Michigan's other bishops. He complained of a stiff neck and headaches. His staff insisted he see a doctor, a visit I arranged at Saint Mary's. An MRI and physical therapy were ordered. He missed several church meetings across the Diocese and asked his Vicar General, Bill Duncan, and Chancellor, Sister Patrice Konwinski, to act in his name. Kevin rested at home insisting that "this too shall pass." It did not. It was a far different kind of door God was about to ask him to walk through.

On Saturday May 15th Sister Patrice called Kevin's home to see how he was feeling. There was no answer. She thought he might have turned off his phone so he could rest undisturbed, or perhaps he had driven to Detroit to see his sister. Bill Duncan asked her to investigate. An hour later, she and a diocesan maintenance man entered Kevin's home. There in his bedroom, in the gray light of midmorning, they discovered that he had died. He lay there perfectly still. It was a poignant farewell. And there were suddenly questions in the sadness. How and why did this happen? For the moment it would have to be enough to know that Bishop Britt had simply died peacefully in his sleep. Sister Patrice called Bill Duncan who raced to the house. "It was pretty unbelievable," Bill said.

To fully appreciate Kevin Britt, I must start at the beginning, not the end. I had gotten off to a good start with Bishop Robert J. Rose. He fully embraced Saint Mary's, our role in the community, and the effectiveness of our mission. And when I had the idea to have the Lacks cross blessed by the Pope in Rome (see the chapter titled "An Inspired Journey"), Bishop Rose was only too happy to accommodate me, take up the cause and help make it happen. He wrote some of the early letters and made the necessary calls to the Vatican. The ball was rolling. But then in 2002, Bishop Rose announced his retirement. What to do now?

With Bishop Rose's imminent departure, Pope John Paul II appointed Kevin Britt Coadjutor Bishop. He would work with Bishop Rose for an interim period, and then he would officially become the Tenth Bishop of the Diocese of Grand Rapids. Kevin Britt would be Bishop Rose's ideal successor. He had been an Auxiliary Bishop for the Archdiocese of Detroit, and he had worked at the Vatican as Cardinal Edmund Szoka's secretary. Cardinal Szoka was Mayor of the Vatican City State. Kevin knew everyone in Rome – from the bus boys at his favorite restaurants to shop owners along Via del Corso, from the Vatican's Swiss guards to the Pope himself. Kevin Britt was the kind of man who was well-connected yet humble, outgoing, likeable and caring. Simply put, everyone loved Kevin Britt. When he arrived in Grand Rapids from Detroit, I knew this was the start of something wonderful.

So the cross-blessing project was handed off from Bishop Rose to Bishop Britt. He relished the challenge and worked closely with me and the hospital. That he hit the ground running is an understatement. Within a few short weeks I introduced Bishop Britt to the Saint Mary's community. We celebrated his arrival at a dinner party at my house where we talked about the hospital's role and mission in West Michigan's Catholic community, and we also talked about the blessing of the cross and how to make that happen. Kevin pulled out his little black appointment book and suggested we travel to Rome the first or second week in October 2003. It was very matter-of-fact. He would be our partner. Not to worry. He could help.

Working with Bishop Britt was comfortable and relaxed. It was like I had known him all my life. At the time I had a lot of questions about the Catholic faith. After all, I was an Episcopalian. I wanted to understand the community, my position in it, and the role Saint Mary's played across the Diocese. Bishop Britt helped me see and understand the big picture. I wanted to be the very best CEO I could be, to fully serve the hospital as its worthy leader and to serve God. Bishop Britt was so well informed, so knowledgeable, so connected. He was really in my corner. That the Lord had brought Kevin to Grand Rapids, that He had opened another door for him to walk through, was such a blessing.

"Kevin truly enjoyed meeting people," said Monsignor Bill Duncan, who worked closely with Britt when he was Coadjutor Bishop and later Bishop. "When he came here he immediately started to go out to parishes. He'd show up at parish festivals just to meet the people, to be with people," said Duncan. And he loved meeting strangers. "Once he met a couple in the airport in Grand Rapids and the next week I asked him, 'Where are you going for dinner?' And he'd say, 'I'm going to this family's house. I met them at the airport and they invited me to dinner!'" He was that kind of guy.

Duncan recalls that Britt had no real hobbies. "I did play golf with him once. We were both equally horrible. We went to the Steeple Town Charity Golf Outing and were in the same foursome. We were glad to be paired together so we could only embarrass two other people in addition to ourselves. He was a horrible golfer. But that never stopped him. He just wanted to help the community, to build it up."

As Coadjutor, Bishop Britt was very interested in faith formation, in supporting lay ministers, and working with young people. He really wanted to get to know the priests in the Diocese. "He truly felt that was critical that first year," said Duncan. "He wanted to establish good relationships with the priests."

Bishop Britt proved to be an invaluable asset in Rome for the blessing of the cross, helping to shepherd our Saint Mary's group throughout the maze of Vatican City. "To have someone like Kevin who knew the city so well," said Duncan, "who knew the Vatican like the back of his hand, was just a wonderful experience." Arriving at Saint Peter's Square the morning of October 8, 2003, Bishop Britt was not pleased with our seating. He wanted Jane Lacks and me to be situated right up front and the others to be off to the side near the stage. "Kevin knew a lot of the Swiss guards," said Father Mark Przybysz, who was part of our group of twenty-one. "He just walked up the main steps and talked to a couple guys and arranged for the seating. He wasn't nervous or worried. He just went up and made it happen." And it did happen, thanks to Kevin Britt.

It was a touching moment when he whispered in the Pope's ear introducing Jane Lacks and me. "She is such a dignified woman," said Duncan. "It was wonderful. Thanks to Kevin, we had seats right on the side there to watch it all. It was delightful." When the Pope blessed the cross, it was one of those unforgettable experiences, a cherished moment. We had worked so long to make the trip a reality. It was over in an instant. And where would we be without Kevin Britt?

Kevin's Italian was not masterful but it was enough to get our group through Rome. When people would see Kevin on the street, they would greet him with warm smiles and genuine handshakes. "I pay them to say nice things about me," he joked. He was larger than life, like a rock star.

"He just loved holding court," said Duncan. "He loved gathering around a table with a good bottle of wine, good food, telling stories and laughing. Jesus did much of his ministry sitting around a table. Kevin took that very seriously in his own ministry. You could get a lot done sitting around a table and enjoying people compared to standing behind a lectern and talking."

On the flight back to Grand Rapids, Bill Duncan was told that the Pope had accepted Bishop Rose's retirement and that Kevin would become Bishop upon his return to West Michigan.

"There was a huge snow storm the night before," said Sister Patrice. "One of the worst blizzards in decades. Bishop Britt

always said that bad weather followed him." But on the day of
the Mass, the sun came out—another kind of symbol. As our new
Bishop, he would lead us by exercising three principles: Kindness,
Mercy, and Love. It became his motto and would adorn his coat-
of-arms. He was officially installed as Bishop of the Diocese of
Grand Rapids on October 13, 2003.

The week following Bishop Britt's installation, Bill Duncan gathered his staff together. Awaiting Britt's arrival, they lined
the hallway of the Diocesan office complex on Burton Street and
prepared to greet him with an official "salute." When Bishop Britt
arrived, the staff all applauded. In typical Britt fashion, he took
off his rabat (the outer covering of his one-piece garment) reveal-
ing a T-shirt that said "I'm King of the Hill." Everyone laughed
uncontrollably! So did Bishop Britt. "The irony was that he was
mocking his position," said Duncan. "He was so unpretentious and
humble."

Bishop Britt's impact on the Diocese was dramatic but
short-lived. "We keep him in such a saintly light," said Father
Mark, "probably because he didn't make many tough decisions.
He simply wasn't with us for that long. He didn't have time to
make any enemies. He deserves to be in that good light."

Bishop Britt is remembered for many things, not the least
of which is his quick Irish wit. Once when he was asked to speak
at the conclusion of a long day's event, he stood up, walked to the
lectern, paused and said, "Let's go downstairs and eat!" End of
speech.

"He reminds me of that book, *Don't Sweat the Small Stuff*,"
said Monsignor Duncan. "That was probably his gift to so many
people. Sometimes when you're in the heat of the Diocese, little

things can appear much larger than they really are. He would say, 'That's OK, I'll deal with that.' That could have been his motto, 'Don't sweat the small stuff. It's all small stuff.'"

But Kevin Britt's vision for the future of the Diocese and Grand Rapids was no small stuff. His dream to live in the city next to the Cathedral, to be near the people, was part of that vision. It just made sense to him. He wanted to set an example—that you could live in or near downtown Grand Rapids. And so renovating the rectory became a top priority. It had not been a residence since Bishop Edward Kelly lived there from 1919-1920.

"Once people heard about the plans for the rectory," said Virginia Pitman, Kevin Britt's sister, "money and materials started pouring in to completely renovate the kitchen, install new windows and heating and air conditioning."

But before he could move into the newly renovated rectory and see his dream fulfilled, Kevin Britt suddenly passed away.

An autopsy determined that Bishop Britt died from a rare disease, a swelling of the brain which was the result of an unusual bacterial infection he had contracted weeks before his death. He was 59. He was the youngest Bishop of Grand Rapids to die in office and he had the shortest tenure, only seven months. His funeral Mass was celebrated on May 21, 2004. A torrent of heavy rain descended on Grand Rapids. Bad weather had followed Kevin Britt once again, even now in death.

The irony of Bishop Britt's passing was that he could not attend the installation of the cross atop the Richard J. Lacks, Sr. Cancer Center or live in the rectory that he dreamed would be his home.

"Little did we know," said Bill Duncan, "that when the cross came back from Rome, Kevin would not be with us. It was a beautiful day when the cross was hoisted up. We all had our sunglasses on. Of course we all thought of Bishop Britt. He was supposed to be here. He was the one who really made it happen. I don't think people attending the installation knew how much sadness everyone was experiencing. Where is he, we all asked? He's supposed to be here." I thought of God, that He was crying with us.

More often than not, I think of Kevin Britt and remember him as a shooting star. One sees it, all bright and brilliant and then in an instant, it is gone. He is gone. At Resurrection Cemetery I stood at Kevin's grave asking, "How is this possible?" Over time, painful grief has grown into a glad remembrance. Yet there remains this gnawing ache, knowing that tomorrow always outlives yesterday, that "time waits for no man," that memory is endless and heals its burden. There is comfort in that, despite the heartache. And I sadly recall with so much gratitude that I knew an angel of the Lord, that I touched his halo, and then he flew away, leaving us with loving memories and, yes, the laughter, always the laughter. Indeed we cast a pebble into the pond. It causes ripples that spread in all directions. Each one of our thoughts, words and deeds is like that. That is how Kevin Britt lived and how he wanted us to live our lives. To cast a pebble into a pond.

The Man for All Seasons

Paul Farr, M.D.

*"If the elevator to success is out of order, you'll have to take the stairs,
one step at a time."*

-Joe Girard

When he was twelve years old and living with his family in Buenos Aires, young Paul Farr experienced one of those "teachable moments" that affected his life forever. He mistreated a maid. "I just yelled at her! My mother called me over and there was hell to pay for what I had done. I get chills just thinking about it," Farr recalls like it was yesterday.

"Your position in life is an accident of birth," she told her son. "You could be the butler or the maid. Don't ever forget that."

Farr remembers that he had to apologize to the maid. "It was a learning experience that I never forgot," he said. "It taught me that no superior has the right to treat anyone like that, absolutely none, zero. And I've kept that close to this day." That one enduring experience set in motion a life of service, generosity and caring for people and helped define Paul Farr, M.D. And so it was no accident that he grew up to be a doctor, a healer, and to treat people kindly and with respect.

The incident in Buenos Aires still haunts him: the unforgiving look in his mother's eyes, the tone of her voice, the stern tongue lashing, and his sheepish apology to the innocent maid. It has stayed with him all his life. It evolved into a simple Golden Rule by which Paul Farr lives every day and with which he measures others: Everyone, regardless of their station in life, who they are or where they come from, deserves to be treated with respect. It helped form his adult values. In some respects, it's why he is so revered in our community and why he has become Saint Mary's "Man for All Seasons." Farr's mother was right and he is better for it, and so are we. It is the stuff of angels.

When the late autumn sun rises in Connecticut's distant eastern sky, it is as red as fire on the verge of the horizon. Calm and unspoiled, Mystic is waking up. "Mystic"—it sounds like an imaginary place in a Sinclair Lewis novel. This was Paul Farr's boyhood home. Just a stone's throw from Long Island Sound in Connecticut's "quiet corner," Mystic is antique and established. Settled in 1684, now, as then, the village exudes a quaint New England charm. It is a safe harbor for tall ships, gorgeous vistas and peaceful seascapes. It is like stepping back in time. Old-world shops and boutiques across the adjoining boroughs, as the travel brochures say, "drip with flowers from window boxes packed cheek-to-cheek." They describe Mystic as a tourist delight, even a classic wedding destination for amorous couples chasing the Hollywood memory of Bogie and Bacall, who honeymooned here in the spring of 1945.

Mystic and its surrounding area are well-known for their artist colonies. Nearby Old Lyme was nicknamed "The Home of American Impressionism." And so when the first snow falls in late November, Mystic resembles an illuminated plein-air painting come to life, dressed in a dusting of fluffy white, trimmed with colorful holiday pageantry. The images are enduring. The cold sea mist bites and smarts. The wind howls. Time slows down.

People contemplate the moment. And there is a quiet grace to Mystic's beauty, especially at sunrise. Regardless of the season, the region is what celebrated New England poet Mary Oliver might describe as "a blue comma on the map of the world, the emblem of everything."

This is where Paul Farr spent his formative years, in this idyllic maritime province. Mystic was his dwelling place and his private space. For the first time in his young life, Farr was finally grounded by a permanent address. He went to high school in nearby Stonington where he was voted "Most Likely to Succeed" and selected as "Most Intelligent." He was Mr. Everything— president and valedictorian of his senior class, yearbook editor, a member of the National Honor Society and Student Council, French, math, chess and dramatics clubs, science fair, chorus and more. In 1964 he was off to Harvard and later to Boston University Medical School. He took the stairs, one step at a time.

But before landing in Mystic, Paul Farr's storied grand tour reads like a classic novella. He was born in Chile and was reared by his parents and a young nanny. His memories of Santiago are vague. "I remember my grandfather," he said. "He was an internist. My father was an engineer, and we moved around a lot. I did not have an underprivileged upbringing, in fact quite the contrary." Santiago was an idyllic place, dubbed "The Little Europe of the Southern Hemisphere."

When he was five, Paul and his family left Chile and moved to Cleveland. "People would ask me 'how did you get to this country?' And I would say, 'Pan Am!'" The story always earns a chuckle. Farr went to kindergarten, elementary school and then to Cleveland's Monticello Junior High. He took a year off to live in Paris with his family. "By the time I was seven I had been exposed to Spanish, English, French, German and Italian. I remember asking my mom, 'what language am I speaking right now?' She said I was speaking French. I had no idea."

Farr's young life was a montage of experiences as a result of his father's many project engineering assignments—from Chile to Ohio to France, and in 1960 to Argentina where he and his family lived in Buenos Aires for a year. But it was Mystic where Farr's young life was shaped and fashioned and where he learned the value of volunteering by tutoring young students who weren't quite making the grade. "I was taught that if you're given a lot you have to give a lot back," he said. Good advice and good training for "an angel to be."

After high school in Stonington, Paul's pre-med education at Harvard was another one of those impressionable experiences. He graduated in 1968 at the height of Vietnam, joined the Army and served overseas in Southeast Asia. In 1970 he married Bridget Dreyse, who had emigrated to the U.S. from Santiago. Paul first met Bridget during a trip back to Chile when he was twelve. "We didn't exactly get along. She thought I was a spoiled brat." Small world. Bridget's father was Paul's grandfather's attorney. "I had always known the family," said Paul.

With his discharge from the Army in 1970 Farr entered Boston University to study medicine. Located in the city's historic South End, BU's medical school was an ideal match for Farr. Its mission was based on a set of values that mirrored his own: integrity, service, social justice. After all, this was the nation's first university that offered a medical education to women, and it had earned a reputation for equal opportunity, having graduated America's first black woman physician. And BU was dedicated to reaching out to the underserved and Boston's indigent population.

For Paul Farr, this was more than a medical education; it taught him valuable life lessons of serving others, embracing the less fortunate, volunteering, giving back. After graduating in 1974, he interned at the University of Iowa and then specialized in internal medicine and gastroenterology. Fellowships at Iowa and the University of Kansas followed. His *curriculum vitae* began to read like a Who's Who. Eventually, all roads led to Grand Rapids. He arrived here in 1980 and hit the ground running at Saint Mary's Hospital.

"Paul was encouraged to practice in Grand Rapids by local physician Gene Heeringa, who knew Paul at the University of Iowa," said Dr. Bill Passinault, a veteran Saint Mary's surgeon and Chairman of the hospital's Ethics Committee. "Paul eventually became Gene's senior partner at Grand River Gastroenterology. He had a single focus. He's always been a forward thinker and very entrepreneurial. Grand River Gastroenterology became the preeminent pioneering group in the city and had close ties with our surgical group," said Passinault.

I didn't know Paul well but our paths did cross when I was at Butterworth. He was well respected. Everyone thought highly of him. One can't help but like the guy. He made a major impression on Grand Rapids' medical community.

I first got to know Paul at a conference in Reston, Virginia that had convened to discuss physician hospital organizations or PHOs. We were really struggling with the concept of what that meant. I was still at Butterworth and was really a competitor of Saint Mary's.

In the 1990s, physician hospital organizations, were receiving wide attention across the nation. We went all over the country, and I got to see Paul and experience him in these kinds of settings. He was amazing and, to this day, he tends to have all the right leadership qualities. The man amazes me. He's everywhere and he is able to cross incredible barriers.

Paul remembers well the failed merger of Saint Mary's and Blodgett back in 1990. At the time he was Vice Chief of Staff and served on the Board of Trustees at the hospital. "Saint Mary's and Blodgett was a natural partnership," Farr said. "But the merger was doomed only to have Rich DeVos come up with this idea years later, which resulted in Spectrum Health." Bill Passinault was Chief of Staff at the time. "It's unfortunate that the merger didn't happen. It would have provided some balance in the community that is lacking now," said Passinault.

During the 1990s, Saint Mary's had a revolving door with regard to its CEOs. "I was in on every one of those hires," said Farr. "I was very upset when David Ameen left with only two weeks notice. At the time I was Chairman of the Board of Trustees. I thought he was putting the organization at risk. We had no succession plan. It was just a mess." Farr was also involved in dismissing some of Saint Mary's CEOs. "I think he and I took that on in the best interest of the institution," said Passinault. "Until we hired Phil, Saint Mary's CEOs lacked a sense of continuity. They only stayed two or three years unlike executives at Butterworth or Blodgett who had long histories at their hospitals."

When I learned that David Ameen was leaving Saint Mary's it was quite easy to have a conversation with Paul about my coming over from Butterworth. Eventually, I was selected to be Saint Mary's next CEO from a list of very good candidates. But without Paul Farr and also Sister Maurita Sengelaub in my corner, I would have missed the window of opportunity at the hospital. To this day I am indebted to them both, and also to Bill Passinault for their faith in me, and to God for leading me to Saint Mary's Health Care.

Paul made it so easy for me to be successful and for Saint Mary's to thrive. He is a visionary and has always been one of my biggest advocates and an eager supporter of Catholic health care. I recognized right away that Saint Mary's had way too much on its plate. They were trying to be everything to everyone. So my idea was to focus on specific centers of excellence and work in concert with the medical staff; it was Paul Farr who helped facilitate that structure. He functioned almost like a lobbyist for Saint Mary's, a consultant. He knows everything and everyone. He's so well connected. He's a past president of the Michigan State Medical Society so he has access to people in politics and decision-makers in Lansing and Washington, D.C. He is just incredibly tuned in. "I guess the term 'Renaissance Man' really applies to Paul," Bill Passinault said. "It's amazing that he can keep so many balls in the air. But 'Man for All Seasons' really says it all, I think."

In 2007 Paul was instrumental in helping me create a physician's advisory council. At the time, Grand Rapids' medical community was rather unsettled. With the economy in the doldrums, doctors were debating the advantages of becoming employees of hospitals. Spectrum Health was looking at this as well. I asked Paul if he would serve on a council that would help sort out the issues for physicians and help us move forward and accomplish our goals. So this all really started with Paul.

He and I envisioned a physician-administration collaboration where each partner listens to the other. Usually a hospital's administration is at odds with doctors. But that's not how we wanted this to work. We listened. We didn't always agree, but we listened, and we were very blessed to have Paul's insight, which helped make the partnership work.

That organization of doctors evolved into Saint Mary's Physician Organization. We call it "CarePath Partners" and Paul was its first chair. Its mission is to improve care coordination between providers so that the delivery of care all works together. The leadership that Paul provided was just phenomenal. To continue the coordination between the physicians and the hospital, we created a physician hospital organization called the Strategic Alignment Organization. Its mission is to create common strategic priorities between physicians and the hospital. Paul sits at that table, too. He's everywhere. That's why I call him a "Man for All Seasons."

My philosophy was to lead from a position of strength. With our doctors and Saint Mary's administration, indeed the whole was larger than the sum of its parts. That was a real advantage in moving the organization forward. I wanted to gather together many diverse elements and talent. If I was the quarterback, I wanted to make everyone part of the team. When you're leading big organizations, whether it's the state medical society or Saint Mary's or the Grand Rapids Symphony, you need to engage your membership, all the players and all the various instruments that play together to create beautiful music. That was my vision and Paul Farr's too.

Paul became a major cheerleader and advocate for Saint Mary's values and for our people. "Keeping our values in front of us is key," said Farr. "The fact that we are faith-based helps us a lot. Our Board of Trustees is very good at making sure we honor and practice those values. For Grand Rapids to succeed, we need several successful groups. We want Spectrum Health and Metro Health Hospital to be successful. The worst thing for Saint Mary's would be that they fail. I think it's flattering that Spectrum Health has adopted Saint Mary's cancer model. How nice is that!"

When Paul Farr first came to Saint Mary's in 1980, he believed he was very fortunate. Within six months he became the coordinator of our internal medicine residency program. So he got to know our residents. That led him to become Chair of the hospital's medical education program, and in 1990 he was elected Vice Chief of Staff and later Chief of Staff. So he was involved from day one.

In addition to the medical side of Saint Mary's, Farr was also interested in the management side. "You can never learn too much," he always said. He doesn't have an MBA but he might as well have. He began to take courses in management; he read over seventy-five books on the subject. Asked to describe the Paul Farr School of Business, he said "engage as many people as you can."

One book in particular made a lasting impression on Paul: Robert Putnam's *Bowling Alone: The Collapse and Revival of American Community*, which advances the concept of "social capital." It changed Paul's outlook on management and leading people. "Let's say you and I know a person and that person wants to do something," said Farr. "You and I go and introduce that person to someone who might help him succeed. And we gain nothing out of this. We gain nothing in return. That is what building social capital is all about—helping someone else succeed and expecting nothing in return."

"Social capital is based on a set of mutual obligations that are often embedded in the values of a community and on the norms of what is called reciprocity," according to Putnam. "I'll do this for you now with the expectation that you, or someone else, will return the favor," he writes. It is what Tom Wolfe referred to in his novel *The Bonfire of the Vanities: A Novel* as 'the favor bank.' But perhaps no one offered a more succinct definition of reciprocity than Yogi Berra: "If you don't go to somebody's funeral, they won't come to yours."

Paul views Grand Rapids as a social capital kind of community. It's what makes our city special. "When I say to someone, 'you're going to like this person, give him an hour of your time,' and then the two of them strike up a deal, then I come out looking good in both people's estimation," said Paul. "That's social capital. So when I need something from either one of these people that I brought together, both of them are going to say, 'sure, let me help you.'"

Paul Farr is sold on social capital—earning it and spending it. "This works for any organization," he said. "It allows you to move an organization in directions it may not want to go. It works in surprising ways. You never know where or how it's going to help you."

Social capital is something I came to embrace as well. Living and working in Grand Rapids exemplifies that. I knew someone in every corner of the city. So did Paul. We were able to get many things done because we could call on a number of people. Building social capital allows you to be a more effective leader. "When you're only out for yourself, you become very transparent," said Farr. "It's very obvious what you're about, and people will shy away from that. Medical schools do not teach students about social capital. They don't teach you finance or how to read a billing statement. They don't teach bedside manner. Some doctors just don't want to be bothered with that."

Like Paul Farr, I believe Grand Rapids is a first-class medical community. Saint Mary's cares about patients. It cares about the people who live in our city. What Saint Mary's believes is what Paul Farr first learned back at Boston University: to practice excellence, to embrace integrity, to serve, to believe in social justice, collegiality and equal opportunity. That is our mission as well. At Saint Mary's, this is what we teach our doctors, and we get to keep the best doctors that we train. It's a wonderful tradition.

And we are all better because of Paul Farr. He is truly one of Saint Mary's angels! He's given so much of his time. His contribution exceeds any monetary value we could place on it. He's such a dear friend, such an angel among us.

The Kid From Pewamo

Michael J. Jandernoa

"The very essence of leadership is that you have a vision. It's got to be a vision you articulate clearly and forcefully on every occasion. You can't blow an uncertain trumpet."
-Theodore Hesburgh

Everybody is somebody from someplace. For Mike Jandernoa, someplace was Pewamo, Michigan, a provincial village in rural Ionia County 50 miles east of downtown Grand Rapids. It was here that Mike spent his formative years, with experiences that helped form the foundations of his adulthood, lessons that would remain with him forever, a coming of age that to this day he can trace back to this pastoral place. And so John Cougar Mellencamp's famous song, "Small Town," could have been written about Mike Jandernoa. In the song, Mellencamp describes growing up in a small town where he was educated, taught to fear Jesus, and daydream. And he cannot forget the people who loved him and let him be just what he wanted to be in the small town.

When Pewamo was established in 1859 as a station along the Detroit, Grand Haven and Milwaukee Railway, "settlers were lured to this valley by the rolling hills, lush with vegetation." The nearby Grand River that flowed through Lyons Township ran "with a force that promised water power for mills with depth enough for navigation." The village of Pewamo that took root, grew up, and adopted its name from a prominent Native American chief who befriended the white settlers who hunted and fished in the fertile river valley.

The Jandernoa family moved to Pewamo from Detroit in the early 1950s. Mike's father and mother, Don and Patricia, joined Don's brother on the family dairy farm just north of town. For Mike, growing up in this small Midwestern borough was an adventure inspired by its sense of place, by the woods, the river, the nearby hills and valleys, and the abundant fruitful fields. For Mike, Pewamo was the first and the last good country, a place that minds its own business and remains one of Michigan's quintessential small towns.

Identified by the name Pewamo across its steel-plated silvery skin, the town water tower rises like a monolith near the village park. It is visible for miles around and stands tall and true like a reassuring arm around Pewamo's shoulder. The only thing missing is the proverbial smiley face. The Goodtime Bar and Grill has become a habitual gathering place for weekend revelers and Michigan State alumni. Another attraction—the Oakwood Lounge on East Main—is popular among the locals for its Friday night fish fries, live bands, dancing and rousing celebrations.

In Pewamo, everybody knows everybody, their business and probably their secrets, too. The street names are solid and Midwestern: Main, State, Jefferson and Lincoln. Union Bank is a safe haven for Pewamo citizens' money. Chevy and Ford pickup trucks navigate the village streets, the surrounding dusty country roads, and the Bluewater Highway just south of town. An occasional horse-drawn Amish buggy sashays through town. For sure, Pewamo is full of history and consumed by the essence of its past;

there is strength in that. Call it pride. Black and white photos displayed in the local bar reflect a bygone era. Even as young people moved away to the big cities to seek their fortunes, local school children learned that no matter where they roam, Pewamo will always be home. "They will always be from Pewamo."

Like everywhere else, the Depression took its toll here. Unemployment was rampant. But food was never as scarce as it was in the larger cities. The family farms survived and sustained the region, the destitute and the hungry. Pewamo always took care of its own. After World War II, life gradually turned around, and the village blossomed as a feeder town for places like Ionia, Lansing, Lowell and Grand Rapids. But farming was king. Above all, Pewamo remained essentially an agrarian community that never forgot its historical roots.

His friends and acquaintances, and there are many, will tell you that it was Pewamo where Mike Jandernoa learned about those American roots – family, faith, community and hard work. This was a town of good people, and the Jandernoas were among them. Mike's grandfather was the township's veterinarian. Always a life force and a role model to his children, Mike's father, Don, a revered and decorated WWII pilot, was a fervent believer in higher education. But hard work was Mike's first real teacher. Everything he learned growing up here was an initiation to his adolescence and adulthood to come, values like humility, service, volunteering and giving back.

"Mike used to get up early and milk the cows," said his friend Terry Moore, who's known Mike since high school. "Perhaps that's where his sense of duty comes from and his work ethic. His values are rooted in faith and family. He's the kid from Pewamo!"

The kid from Pewamo learned early on that hard work pays off. Yes, talent counts but outworking everyone else has its rewards. "After he graduated from college, Mike used to work the equivalent of fifteen months a year," said Moore.

As a boy who rose with the rooster's crow, who milked his uncle's cows twice a day and dutifully did his chores, Mike learned a great lesson about achieving success. In the words of Abigail Van Buren, "if you want a place in the sun, you've got to put up with a few blisters." Mike's close friend, Russ Visner, who worked with him at Seidman, agrees that hard work pays off. "There's only one way Mike makes it all happen and that's because he works at it. He manages his time and fulfills his commitments, but to do that there are long days."

In Pewamo, the Jandernoas were active and committed members of St. Joseph's Catholic Church. Mike received a traditional parochial school education that helped build the foundation for his later accomplishments. When he was nine years old, the family left Pewamo for Ionia, just 12 miles west on M-21, where they lived for two years before moving to Grand Rapids. Mike's grandfather was dying of cancer so his uncle took over the farm. "When we were in Ionia, I would still go out and help my Uncle Bill on the farm," said Mike. "I'd go out there for long weekends. I'd drive the tractors, the trucks and so forth."

His Catholic education made a lasting impression. "Back in the 1950s a lot of Catholic boys dreamed of becoming priests. It was an important calling," said Moore. When he was fourteen, Mike spent a year at Saint Joseph Seminary in Grand Rapids studying for and pondering the priesthood. Faith, religion and the church were very important to him. But he was drawn more to the secular world. "I prayed on it," said Jandernoa. "I'm glad I made the change."

His decision not to pursue the priesthood was a major turning point in Mike's life. With a new direction, he transferred to Grand Rapids' Catholic Central High School. "He was an all-around good guy," Moore recalls. "He was a triple threat: a great athlete, a standout student and a superior leader. And he was such a well-liked guy. He had that affability quotient to him."

During the summers of 1967 and 1968 Mike worked at Saint Mary's Hospital as a janitor and a painter. "That experience got me acquainted with how hospitals worked," Mike said. Even during the riots of 1967 Mike walked to his job at the hospital from the family home near Grand Rapids' Garfield Park. "I didn't have any money so I walked or hitchhiked," he said. On two occasions, Sister Mary Maureen McDonald, then Saint Mary's Hospital Administrator, picked Mike up and scolded him for walking the streets during the riots. "But I figured I could outrun anyone. So that was my first exposure to Saint Mary's," said Mike.

Looking back on his high school years at Catholic Central, Mike will say that one thing stands out above everything else. He met and dated Sue Zoellner. "Mike was in the Class of 1968 and Sue in 1969," said Russ Visner, who knew Sue at Catholic Central. "I think she and Mike got married the year before she graduated from college." Sue was an education major at Central Michigan University and taught in the East Grand Rapids school system for over 25 years. Mike calls Sue "a blessing." She is his soul mate and his sounding board, the glue that holds everything together in their lives. "She been terrific over the years," Mike said. Sue's family belonged to Immaculate

Heart of Mary. "Ever since they've been married, they've attended IHM," said Visner.

After two semesters at the University of Detroit, Mike transferred to the University of Michigan to study accounting. "I used to see Mike at the business school library," said fellow Wolverine, Terry Moore. "He was always there studying. That impressed me. I wanted to be just like Mike."

After graduating from Michigan in 1972, Mike passed all five CPA board exams. That was an unheard of accomplishment for a graduating college senior. In short order he landed a job at Seidman and Seidman in Grand Rapids. "He was an exceptional auditor," said Visner. "He was involved in the Old Kent audit and the Amway and Perrigo audits. Those were really key engagements. That's when he got to know John Canepa at Old Kent."

At Seidman volunteering in the community was an essential requirement for employment. Mike plugged into Grand Rapids' Catholic schools, which was experiencing financial challenges.

"We literally had to make phone calls to get enough cash on a Friday so the schools could open on Monday," Mike said. He first served on the school board when he was only 24 years old.

"I've worked on fundraising for over 40 years," said Mike. "It seems like forever."

"The secondary schools could very well have closed," said Visner. "Mike was on the financial end of it and ultimately became president of the school board. He worked very diligently. He always gave of his time and talent. At that time he didn't have any extra money, but he gave his all to the secondary schools."

Mike worked at Seidman for seven years. In 1979, John Canepa called him in for a chat. "I thought 'What's the CEO of Old Kent Bank calling me over for? It was kind of off-season for the bank audit,'" said Mike.

Canepa was direct and very determined. "Why the hell are you an accountant?" he asked. "You're a talented guy. You should be a businessman. You ought to go out and find yourself a job as a chief financial officer for a firm."

The firm Canepa had in mind was Perrigo, which grew to become the nation's largest manufacturer and marketer of store brand, over-the-counter drug and nutritional products. "John kind of facilitated Mike's getting the job there as the company's CFO. He thought Mike was management material," said Visner.

"I would never have gone to Perrigo had John not sat me down and advised me," Mike said. "He told me if things didn't work out, I could always come back and be a partner at Seidman."

His career at Perrigo was stellar. With Canepa's endorsement, Mike was hired as its CFO in 1979 and promoted to Executive Vice President of Sales and Finance in 1981, President in 1983 and CEO in 1986, and finally Chairman of the Board and CEO in 1991, a position he held until May of 2000. During his Perrigo career, he led two leveraged buyouts and the company's Initial Public Offering (IPO) in 1991. During his time at Perrigo, Mike took the company from a privately held $30 million company to a $2.5 billion publicly traded firm.

Perrigo's leveraged buyout might not have happened had it not been for Mike's friendship with John Canepa and Old Kent Bank. "John took a big risk. He really stuck his neck out. But in the end it paid off for Perrigo and our employees," said Mike.

"Mike was a good negotiator, a great customer relations type guy," said Canepa. "He went through some tough times at Perrigo. But he stuck by it and did a good job growing that company."

I first met Mike in the early 1990s when I was still at Butterworth. We were both part of a YMCA program called "Indian Guides," today known as "Adventure Guides." It has a long history of helping dads spend some quality time with their sons and daughters. Mike's son and my son were about the same age. Our families lived in the same Cascade neighborhood. Urged by a mutual friend to get involved, both Mike and I plugged into the program.

"We would go to various Y-camps," said Mike. "There were activities we'd do with our sons over long weekends, things like hiking, canoeing, arts and crafts and making vests and headdresses. It was a good time, a great experience. The kids had a blast!" And so did the dads! Mike and I bonded as much as our sons. It is a lifelong friendship that began in the Michigan woods at places like Camp Manitou-lin along the shores of Barlow Lake.

About the same time I left Spectrum Health, Mike was beginning to interface with Saint Mary's where he got more involved. Mike had been asked to help out with fundraising for the Lacks Cancer Center. The campaign attracted Mike because he had had a family experience with cancer. His mother Patricia died from the disease in 1994 and was buried in the family plot in Pewamo.

"Before the Lacks Cancer Center project, I had been involved with a couple of events at Saint Mary's," Mike said. "But it wasn't a long term commitment. But being a Catholic Central graduate, I would naturally have gravitated toward Saint Mary's." His first exposure to the hospital came when he was fourteen. He broke his leg playing football for Saint Francis Parish and was in traction for a week.

The Lacks family's experience at MD Anderson in Houston, where Dick Lacks, Sr. was treated for cancer in 1999, left quite an impression on Dick Lacks, Jr. in terms of what he wanted to see done. Dr. Tom Gribbin's association with the project was instrumental and helped persuade Mike to get involved. Dick Lacks, Sr. died that same year. (See the chapter titled "An Inspired Journey"). "Dr. Gribbin embodied, to me, what patient-centered care is all about," said Mike. "He is a spectacular doctor. He really envisioned the cancer center. He's so patient-focused. And then we had the confidence of having Phil McCorkle as Saint Mary's CEO, and so there was a lot of passion there for the cancer center. With the two of them, I became convinced that this would be very special."

Mike and Sue Jandernoa, Ken and Noreen Hungerford, John and Nancy Kennedy, and Dick Lacks and served as fundraising co-chairs. This most successful campaign raised over $45 million in private money for the Lacks Cancer Center. At the time, it was the largest private donor project in Grand Rapids' history. After doing the moral arithmetic, Mike and Sue Jandernoa personally wrote a generous check.

"I've been blessed in my life," said Mike. "From a Catholic perspective, we are asked to give back, and so we have a responsibility to share what we have and give based on our own means."

And taking care of the less fortunate was part of the Catholic equation as well. "Serving the underserved, the homeless was what I thought the Catholic community needed to do. That mission is beyond just making money in a hospital setting," said Mike. "To me that is an important part of being a human being."

Mike's friend, Terry Moore, agrees. "Mike's always been a 'giver.' It's kind of a cliché but that is Mike. For him, it's not about what you have done but what you can give. That comes out of his faith experience. It's a sign of Mike's humanity. It means you are always part of something bigger."

And Mike has another old school value that was taught to him by his parents and the Catholic Church back in Pewamo. Never say anything negative about another person. "I've never heard Mike say a mean word about anybody. He has a tremendous self-discipline. If you don't have anything good to say about someone, don't say it," said Moore.

Mike and Sue Jandernoa's commitment to Saint Mary's is solid. Following the Lacks Cancer Center campaign, they generously supported building the Hauenstein Neuroscience Center and helped back Saint Mary's Sophia's House project. For Mike, health care in Grand Rapids is not about competing but about serving, "how you treat others in the community, serving patients with special needs," Mike said.

"I never thought much about leaving Grand Rapids," said Mike. "I always thought this was a special and unique community. Here business leaders are expected to be involved in the community. I like that aspect, that we as a business community have an obligation besides just making money. Grand Rapids is special. We are blessed."

Mike's relationship to Saint Mary's has been wonderful. Without him, where would we be? He's a real champion for the hospital. His style and personality have never really changed. He's so kind. He's a very strong Catholic. And he's a great advisor to me. He will always tell me where the trouble spots are, where to step and where not to step. He's dealt with everyone in

Grand Rapids. He knows everyone! I can always pick up the telephone, and he can always call me. He often does, just to chat or to tell me something that I should know.

"One of Mike's sports heroes is Larry Bird," said Moore. "Before the Detroit Pistons came along, it was the Boston Celtics. That was our team. Bird had great qualities. He had great court vision. He could almost see people behind him, if they were trailing him. He had tremendous eyesight. Mike has that same kind of ability as a leader. He has great vision. He can see all the various community players and how they fit together. He's very perceptive. Bird always inspired his teammates to play better. Mike is like that too. We all want to be better because we admire Mike so much."

From his office on the 8th floor of Bridgewater Place, Mike Jandernoa has an expansive view of downtown Grand Rapids. Dressed in a coat and tie, he slowly sips a glass of water and scribbles notes on a yellow legal pad. From where he sits, he can envision it all, the seen and unseen institutions he has influenced for the greater good of Grand Rapids and beyond: the Van Andel Institute, the Michigan State University College of Human Medicine, the Medical Mile, Grand Valley State University, Fifth Third Bank, Hope on the Hill, Aquinas College, the Michigan Life Science Corridor, Grand Action, the Michigan Economic Development Corporation, and in the distance to the south and to the east, Catholic Central High School, the Cathedral of Saint Andrew and Saint Mary's Health Care.

"The largest population in Kent County is Catholic," said Mike. "So Saint Mary's has a niche—to take care of Catholic patients, no question. To me, part of that aspect is that Catholic

Central is located downtown. And Saint Mary's is downtown. The Cathedral is downtown. To me that has always been the center of our faith. And part of your faith is your health and especially in the last phases of your life. That's all part of that whole Catholic experience."

Mike is a man of great faith—faith in God; faith in and loyalty to his friends; faith in our city; our state; the nation; and certainly faith in Saint Mary's Health Care. He is not afraid to show it. Subtly, God is always there. Before a meal, public or private, he will always say grace and make the sign of the cross.

Like the Bible parable, Mike has built his life on a firm foundation. When the storms in his life have come, his rock is strong, supported by four great pillars that sustain him – family, faith, community and service, all tempered by hard work.

Nearly 40 years ago, John Canepa recognized a rising star in Mike Jandernoa. Always on the ascent, that star has never stopped rising. Since leaving Perrigo in 2003, greater Grand Rapids has been the benefactor of his entrepreneurial passion: Bridge Street Capital Management, the Jandernoa Investment Group, Grand Angels and now JEM (Jandernoa Entrepreneurial Mentoring), an enterprise he and Sue founded in 2010 devoted to mentoring small businesses and to help enterprising entrepreneurs expand their companies.

On a bright spring day, against a cloudless sky, solitary and silhouetted, he strikes a youthful pose against his office windows facing south. His eyes peer into the deep horizon, where the sun rises. As far as his mind's eye can see, as far as his imagination and memory take him, there lies Pewamo, 50 miles to the east of downtown Grand Rapids, the village of his youth, where it all began—his introduction to the world.

Today, Pewamo is a mere shadow of its former self, yet it cannot escape its colorful past. Over time, it has lost the core of its population, which once numbered nearly 700; by 2010 it had dwindled to just 469, according to the latest census. Short of farming and family, there is not much here to keep an enterprising son or daughter grounded. But for those who have stayed or who have migrated here to live, Pewamo is home, what American writer Washington Irving called "that paternal hearth, that rallying place of the affections."

The imagination plays out in Pewamo. For Mike, the mind wanders. In Saint Joseph's Cemetery just south of town, in the dreary light of a gray midmorning, there is the family plot, the deceased resting in the consolation of numbers among the ancients and more recent burials. Here, the Jandernoas are plenty and prominent – William and Paul, Elizabeth and Anthony, and Mike's mother, Patricia. As the poet Edgar Lee Masters wrote, "They are all sleeping, sleeping, sleeping on the hill."

Yes, we are all somebody from someplace. Our life is like time seen through the lens of the past. Our coming of age shapes us; so do the people we love and who love us. We cannot forget them. "To be good is noble," wrote Mark Twain, "but to show others how to be good is nobler yet." Just ask the kid from Pewamo.

Working Together Toward Holiness

Nancy and John Kennedy

"We are each of us angels with only one wing, and we can fly only by embracing one another."

-Luciano de Crescenzo

It was a warm summer morning in northeast Grand Rapids. At the end of an inconspicuous cul-de-sac, a well-worn asphalt driveway bordered by lush green grass and open spaces makes its way toward the Kennedy home. The silence is broken by a dog barking; Nancy appears at the front door with a warm welcoming smile, sparkling eyes and a firm handshake. She shushes the dog and proceeds to the living room.

"John and I met at the University of Detroit Mercy, even though he is three years older than I am and he graduated in three years. He fast-tracked college, since he was paying for it himself," Nancy said.

When I first came to Saint Mary's in the spring of 2000, I asked John to serve on our hospital board, but he turned me down. Instead, he offered Nancy's service. It remains one of John's greatest gifts to our hospital.

"Nancy understands things at a different level than a lot of people. If you want something done diplomatically, you don't send me in. It's not my natural style. Most people would say that my bedside manner is a bit more edgy than hers," said John.

"John was employed at Deloitte in Grand Rapids," said friend and admirer, Joe Schmieder, former chairman of the Saint Mary's Foundation. "While he and Nancy were dating, John went to Autodie, where he was appointed CFO at the age of 23. Part of his job was to manage a small start-up called Autocam, and when the owner decided to spin off the company, John was able to buy it, and he built the company. That's where his financial acumen comes in. John leveraged everything he had to buy and grow the business."

The rest, as they say, is history. Today Autocam is an exemplary global enterprise reflecting, above all, John Kennedy's entrepreneurial instincts, talent and confidence.

From the very beginning, Nancy was impressed with Grand Rapids. "I would drive over from Detroit and when I got in range, I would listen to the radio. You could always tell, even on the radio, that this was a very positive, upbeat place," she said.

John credits Father James Cusack as having made a major impact on his spiritual life. "I was having a fair amount of success financially when I first met Fr. Cusack at Saint Thomas Parish. He pulled me aside one day and asked me what I was doing. This was before Nancy and I got married. He saw this young guy, and he mentored me. From a philosophical aspect, Fr. Cusack taught me that nothing we have is ours. We're just temporary custodians of these resources while we are on earth. So I started trying to figure out what I was supposed to do with these gifts. How do I use my time, treasure and talent?"

Nancy and John first got involved with the hospital through Dick Lacks. "Dick is one of the biggest-hearted people around," said John.

"John saw what Dick's family went through with regard to cancer. Dick asked us to help lead the campaign to fund the building of the Richard J. Lacks, Sr. Cancer Center. I was asked to serve on the hospital board after the campaign, and that's how I got plugged in," said Nancy.

Saint Mary's Micki Benz believes Nancy really took the board in a different direction because she pushed hard for appropriate governance.

"Hospital governance requires participation by people from the non-medical community," said Nancy. "It's very important for board members to feel that they can safely ask questions."

Over time, Nancy became board chair at Saint Mary's. She has always asked the deep, penetrating questions. "What distinguishes a Catholic hospital from a non-Catholic hospital?" she asks. "We need to be able to answer that question for others."

I always appreciated Nancy's extraordinary preparation for board meetings. She was tenacious, and her leadership style with board work was very effective. She believed Saint Mary's deserved her utmost attention and commitment.

"Saint Mary's doesn't benefit if board members are not engaging in meaningful dialogue and it's a bad use of people's time to sit in a meeting. If everyone in the room simply agrees, that's a waste of people's time, too. So as chair, I really worked hard to build the type of environment where everyone is actively involved," Nancy said.

"All serve all," she believes. "That is Saint Mary's."

For John, Saint Mary's Health Care is all about the mission.

"I think Saint Mary's is doing a really good job of providing and meeting a community need," he said. "I think the concept of trying to figure out ways to provide spiritual as well as physical healing is really good. There's a spirit that's different at Saint Mary's, and part of that is because of who they are."

Looking back on his life, John recalls that his parents took volunteering very seriously. "My father's parents didn't get to go to college," said John, "and my dad really pushed the value of education. He was always volunteering and always working to improve himself."

In addition to hard work and volunteering, Nancy and John are defined by their generosity. "The Kennedys are incredibly generous," said Schmieder.

Sometimes John and Nancy ponder their giving. "It's easy to give money to an organization, but are those organizations going to be responsible in doing the Lord's work and in carrying out their mission? How do you make sure they continue to do that?" said John. "It just makes sense to give as much as you can, but the reality is that we're just trying to be good stewards."

John made his first "major" gift to his alma mater, the University of Detroit, immediately after he graduated. "They had this group called the President's Cabinet, which cost $1,000 to join, and Deloitte, where I worked, had a matching gift program so I would renew every year," said John. The President's Cabinet generated competitive academic scholarships for students. "And what is really ironic is that Nancy was one of the recipients of the scholarship!"

Nancy's tenure on Saint Mary's board and her time as board chair made a lasting impression, both on her and the hospital. "Boards are nothing without a leader who has a vision. Things happen when someone has a vision that is good enough to convince other people to go along with it. The board's role is governance, to put the right people in place, to provide different perspectives." Under Nancy's watch, board work flourished.

Nancy and John Kennedy are a team. Like John, Nancy is philosophical. "We have such extremes in health care to work out as a society," said Nancy. "People drink excessively, smoke, and do all sorts of unhealthy things, but then we all want to be healthy. This calls into question what the expectation should be, what care is and should be, and yet, the health care system doesn't judge, they just try to compassionately live up to their philosophy which asks people to expect something more."

Stepping down from the board at Saint Mary's, Nancy has learned a lot about health care. One of the things she will miss most is the progress she experienced during her tenure. "The medical field has made such great strides in the quality of care it delivers," she said.

Grand Rapids is home. "There is such an underlying faith in God in this community, which calls us to look beyond ourselves," said Nancy. "The question is whether we will maintain that attitude. I think that will determine the future of the city's philanthropic calling."

Unprofoundly Profound

Robert L. Herr

"Do not let loyalty and faithfulness forsake you; bind them around your neck, write them on the tablet of your heart."

-Proverbs 3:3

When legendary UCLA basketball coach John Wooden compiled his philosophy of leadership, he might have had fellow Hoosier, Bob Herr, in mind. "Ability may get you to the top," said Wooden, "but it takes character to keep you there." More than any other personal quality, character best describes Bob Herr. Truly, "the wings of angels are often found on the backs of the most unlikely people," said Eric Honeycutt. "All God's angels come to us disguised," quipped James Russell Lowell.

He was born in the spring of 1945 and grew up in South Bend, located in the provincial heartland of northwest Indiana. As a naive youth he ran away from home at sixteen. Herr never dreamed that one day he would direct the office of one of the nation's most successful accounting firms, or that he would become an influential Grand Rapids community leader and an angel to Saint Mary's Health Care.

Along his journey from there to here, Herr transformed himself from a young man to a visionary leader with character.

And it is his character that we admire most, what Abraham Lincoln described as "a tree with reputation as its shadow" or what H. Jackson Brown, Jr. chronicled as "what we do when we think no one is looking." Herr's sense of duty is habitual. It is his passion. His actions mirror his values. Loyalty becomes like a burning candle in dark places. He never forgets his friends. Devotion and reliability illuminate the community with the light of always striving to do the right thing and always for the common good. That is his character shining through. He is the real deal. Responsibility inspires boundless hope in him and in others. It seems to epitomize the old adage penned by an unknown author, that, "If all my friends were to jump off a bridge, I would not follow. I'd be at the bottom to catch them when they fall."

For me, Bob Herr is not only a friend but a mentor. He is a counselor and a coach. I am a better person because of him. We are all better people because of him. And Saint Mary's Health Care is a better place because of him.

Few of us measure up to Bob Herr. He stands above all of us. We can only look up to him in wonder. He is high on our list of people we would like to emulate, in whose shoes we would like to walk, to be in his rarefied air. That is a tall order, indeed. True, it was Herr's ability that took him to the top, but it is his character that has kept him there. "Reputation," said Thomas Paine, "is what men and women think of us. Character is what God and the angels know of us."

Formally established in 1835, South Bend is a mere five miles from the Michigan line. It was home to the Studebaker boys, who set up a wagon shop there in 1852 that eventually grew to become one of the world's largest automobile enterprises. The

Singer Sewing Company and Oliver Chilled Plow dominated the city's industrial complex, and the University of Notre Dame, located just north of town, became a major force in the area's economy and culture. In 1934 the Merchants National Bank was the last depository to be robbed by the notorious Dillinger Gang. Then and now the St. Joseph River snakes timelessly from the east end and turns near the city center, thus the name, "South Bend."

The megalopolis of Chicago was only ninety-five miles to the west. In its wake were the fiery furnaces of Hammond and Gary, the picturesque Indiana Dunes along the southern shore of Lake Michigan, and placid communities like LaPorte, Rolling Prairie, and New Carlisle. This was very old land amidst the morning dew and the high corn breezes that cast their fragrance across the fertile fields and beyond. When the storms came in across the Big Lake, young Herr could hear the thunder faintly far off and watch the high dark clouds approaching in the distance over the neighbor's rooftops and through the oak tree leaves. When the winds blew, Herr imagined the tree limbs rubbing against the siding of the tri-level house on Central Drive in the Oakmont Park section of South Bend, driven by the heat of countless Indiana summer suns, flapping like lumbering elephant ears. The rattling sound was predictable and played out like a melodious symphony with the trees and the harmony of the wind gusts. South Bend was a near perfect place to grow up, to dream and trust that life would always turn out as it should, with more pleasure than pain. And it was mostly true. This is how I envisioned Bob Herr's childhood and imagined it as a blending of fact and fiction.

Growing up in the Midwest provided an innocence of both time and place. South Bend was like a native land. It was home, his home. The region was an inspiration, especially for artists and writers, like David Foster Wallace, who described the region as

"flannel plains and blacktop graphs and skylines of canted rust…
where untilled fields simmer shrilly in the A.M. heat."

The summers of the early 1960s were scorchers across
northern Indiana. By mid-afternoon the lazy Hoosier sun above
South Bend was as hot as a blast furnace. For young Bob Herr, life
in South Bend was predictable, innocent and safe. I imagined him
playing board games on the front porch after dinner, pacing himself, sipping a welcome glass of his mother's ice cold lemonade; it
was the only way to escape July's insufferable heat.

His family and his friends call him "Bullet." It was an iron-
ic nickname that fit and stuck because he dealt cards at a snail's
pace. His actions were measured and methodical, deliberate and
easy. The right moves did not come quickly — what Shakespeare
called "Wisely and slow; they stumble that run fast." And so the
moniker "Bullet Bob" stayed with Herr all his life.

Our youthful experiences are like great teachers. Good
and bad, adventures or misadventures, we learn from them and we
remember, and we grow up to be better or worse for them.   The
summer of 1960 was noteworthy: Arnold Palmer won the U.S.
Open, hootenannies were all the rage, Kennedy and Johnson were
nominated by the Democrats to run against the GOP's Nixon and
Henry Cabot Lodge. Four months later Kennedy would prevail
as America's first Catholic president. But one major event that
summer changed Bob Herr forever. He still talks about it. He ran
away from home.

On a hot July afternoon, a high school friend named Paul
decided to leave home. Herr was the only person he told. "He
just wanted to get away," said Herr. "He wanted to go away. So I
said to him that he couldn't just do that, or do it alone, and I said
that I would go with him."

Herr remembers writing a note to his parents: "Gone for a couple of days. I'll be fine. Don't worry." Herr carefully crawled out of his bedroom window and dropped onto the parched yard below. He and Paul disappeared into the searing Indiana dusk and hitched a ride to Diamond Lake near Cassopolis, Michigan. At the end of the evening, they left for Paul's family cottage and walked ten miles east into the dark to Birch Lake, arriving late at night "because nobody would pick us up and give us a ride." They had plans to spend the night at Paul's family cottage but "we couldn't get in so we broke into the cottage next door, spent the night, made breakfast the next morning, cleaned things up and left," said Herr.

The next day, like two mischievous Tom Sawyers out for a joy ride, Bob and Paul hitchhiked west down U.S. 6 all the way to Davenport, Iowa. "We had $10.40 between us," said Herr. Arriving at the banks of the Mississippi River they met up with three or four boys their own age. One was a Samaritan who, upon hearing their story, offered to take Paul and Bob home to spend the night, "and that's what we did," said Herr. It was a Mark Twain moment.

Befriended by the young stranger and his family, the boy's mother "offered to feed us, clean us up and put us up," said Herr, "with the understanding that we would promise to return to South Bend." And so the next day, thanks to a series of kindly truckers, they hitchhiked all the way home to South Bend.

Looking back on the experience, Herr said he ran away because his friend needed a companion. "I didn't want him to be alone. I didn't think it was a good idea for my friend to be by himself." The story has stayed with him for over fifty years, no apologies, no regrets. It was one of those "teachable moments," an introduction to the meaning of life and loyalty, "because of all the things granted us by wisdom, none is greater or better than friendship," wrote Italian poet, Pietro Aretino. Bob Herr had come of age.

The day after he returned to South Bend after his adventure with his friend, Paul, Herr met a girl who had just arrived in town from Hamilton, Ohio. Her name was Barb Iams. "She was new to the neighborhood," he said. If Bob Herr was the town's itinerant Tom Sawyer, Barb quickly became his Becky Thatcher. He was love-struck. "The sun rose upon a tranquil world, and beamed down upon the peaceful village like a benediction," wrote Mark Twain, almost as if he had been there. "He worshipped this new angel with a furtive eye." After meeting Barb for the first time, Herr was never quite the same again, nor was she.

"Barb was the oldest of seven children," said Herr. "She was the queen! Her father was an engineer at Bendix. I went to public school; Barb went to Saint Joseph's Catholic High School." They dated and were inseparable. "But I wasn't Catholic. Her mother wanted Barb to marry a Catholic," he said.

"Barb was able to offer a lot of stability in Bob's life," said Herr's long-time friend, John Benz. "I think it was Barb and maybe her family, too, that gave Bob some direction in his life. Barb is a very devoted Catholic. She's his anchor," said Benz.

"I did a lot of crazy things in high school," said Herr. "But I never really got into trouble, never got arrested. But I sure had my share of fun! I was voted Best Dressed and Homecoming King, but that's because the ballot box got stuffed!"

After high school, Barb went to Holy Cross School of Nursing in South Bend. In 1963 Herr was accepted at Western Michigan University in Kalamazoo where he quickly abandoned his quest to become a geologist ("I liked the idea of working outside, pounding rocks") to pursue business. He was the only member of his family who went to college; he worked as a laborer for a bricklayer to pay for his education. "The accounting stuff seemed to click," said Herr. "I got very good grades in college. I studied a lot, maybe too much. I really had to work hard to achieve something."

After graduating from Western in 1967 with a degree in business, Herr returned to South Bend and went to work for Crowe Chizek. He and Barb were married in August. Barb became an Intensive Care Unit nurse at Saint Joseph's Hospital, now part of Trinity Health, and Herr labored as a proverbial bean-counter at Crowe. "I did not grow up in a Catholic family," Herr said. "We were a little bit of everything – Methodist, Congregational, Protestant. I didn't convert to Catholicism until Barb and I got married."

When Herr started at Crowe there were thirty people in the firm. "They wanted to expand and compete with the larger firms," said Herr. "So I was part of that early growth."

By 1983, Crowe had swelled to a staff of 250 people, having recruited some of the best and the brightest young accountants they could find. Growth created opportunity; Crowe's management recognized Herr's leadership skills and asked him to lead a team of fifteen, move to Grand Rapids and set up an office there. "Initially, it was a shock," said Herr. "We had just designed and built a new house in South Bend. We had a growing family. Barb and I thought we'd be there forever. But she was a real trooper about it. She said, 'OK, let's do this!' And the kids didn't put up a lot of fuss." So the Herr family moved to Grand Rapids – Indiana's loss, Michigan's gain.

Crowe chose Grand Rapids because it was a regional hub. People sought out the city for its high quality goods and services.

It had an established banking and legal community that Crowe used for referrals. "They had a lot of inroads with banks and lumber yards," said John Benz. "That was Crowe's foundation – banking and lumber yards. And now look at Crowe in Grand Rapids! It's all because of Bob and Barb."

When Herr first came to the city, he had one major goal in mind. "I said to myself that I had better meet some people," he recalls. Crowe's first office was in the Commerce Building. So was the local United Way. "I walked into their office and told the director I wanted to get involved. That's how Crowe began to build its brand, through doing volunteer and leadership work. It got our name around. Crowe encouraged everyone on its staff to get involved in the community. They were very supportive of volunteering one's time and leadership."

While Herr volunteered with the United Way, Barb and the Herr children were active in Grand Rapids' Catholic schools where they met lifelong friends the Benzes, Jackoboices, Bradys, Murphys and Sharpes.

"I don't know why but hospitals really interested me," said Herr. "About four years after we moved to Grand Rapids, Saint Mary's board members, John Jackoboice and Katy MacAleenan, encouraged me to serve on the board." Herr immersed himself in the health care field and served the hospital for nine years, two years as Board Chair. "There was a lot of turnover in leadership," said Herr. "Those were tough times for Saint Mary's. It was a struggle."

I first met Bob in 1995 or 1996 about the time when Spectrum Health was being created. I was still at Butterworth. Nancy Hart was Saint Mary's CEO, and Bob was serving on the hospital board. But it wasn't until I began as Saint Mary's President and

CEO in 2000 that I came to fully appreciate Bob Herr. He was a major asset for the hospital and made sure that Saint Mary's always had a seat at the table in Grand Rapids.

Herr's primary focus at Saint Mary's was Advantage Health, which was officially formed in January 1995. Originally known as Family Care, Advantage Health started out with twenty-five physicians in private practice. Those practices were purchased by the hospital; the physicians group had a 50% share in the governance of the business.

"Bob Herr was one of the early community members," said Dr. Dave Blair, President and CMO of Advantage Health. "He was there from the very beginning." Advantage Health's board was chaired either by a physician or by someone from the hospital or community side. "So when it was Saint Mary's turn, they'd always turn it over to Bob," said Blair.

In July 2010 the Advantage Health model evolved again as a wholly-owned non-profit subsidiary of the hospital. "It was always Bob who facilitated the conversation between the hospital and the physicians," said Blair. "Bob was, in a sense, a counselor and a coach. He was also kind of the voice of the patient; he was able to see both sides of the issue, the hospital's and the physicians' points of view."

Herr was always someone who could be trusted. That's what I've always liked about him. He has the trust of both Saint Mary's and the physicians. As Advantage Health evolved, Herr was always the go-to person. He goes everywhere. He and Barb are everywhere, so well connected, always in perpetual motion.

"Bob is not one who just talks," said Dave Blair, M.D. "He also asks a lot of questions to get under the surface to help create a depth of understanding. Like a lot of businesses, health care is very 'siloed.' You have all these little departments that don't always communicate with each other as well as they should. Bob is a creative thinker so he can envision what might be, and he can lead people and help them understand how they might accomplish more," said Blair.

"I thought this health care thing was just huge, hard to move, hard to change," said Herr. "Medicine is really a strange business model. The payers, the providers, the physicians, and the patients, none of these people were connected. But it really got me engaged. I just jumped in. I wanted to learn more. I wanted to make change."

A big part of Herr's success is his work ethic. He simply outworks everyone else. "I still remember a lot of things as a child in South Bend," he said. "On my mother's side, we had a lot of farmers. I was always close to my grandmother. Her husband, my grandfather, was a hard working guy. He had white hair, several tractors, cows, pigs. I remember castrating pigs with my grandfather, razor blade and turpentine. I was always by his side as a little kid on the farm just outside of South Bend. If he went out behind the barn to do his business, I'd be right behind him."

Herr is an indispensable part of Saint Mary's operation. "Bob's a great guy to have on your side when things are going well," said Blair. "He's an even better guy to have on your side when things are tough."

Long time friend, John Benz, attributes much of Herr's success to Barb. "She's a no-nonsense person," said Benz. "Barb is really the CEO in that family. They're a great team."

Benz admires Herr's talent to adapt to any situation. "He's not at all pretentious. He can wade into a circle of total strangers and introduce himself and before you know it, he's conversing with them, telling them things. I think his work ethic is amazing."

But Bob Herr is not perfect. "He's a great strategic planner, but he's not a very good golfer even though he might tell you that he is," said golf partner, John Benz.

Benz describes his friend as a flaky professor. "We were playing golf once, riding in the cart. Bob's got all his stuff but can't find his watch. And I looked over and said, 'Bob, look on your left wrist!' And he burst out laughing. He's very ab-sent-minded. But I think that's why he's been so successful in business. He can sift through all the clutter and get right to what's important. And that's why Bob's been so helpful to Saint Mary's."

Micki Benz, Mercy Health's Vice President of Public Rela-tions and Advocacy for the Trinity Health West Michigan Region, calls Herr 'unprofoundly profound.' "He's not dramatic or intense; he just gets it done. Bob's very logical, not so much emotional, and he is very duty-bound. This is what you do. It's expected. And both he and Barb are very loyal to their friends. That kind of loyalty reflects back to his running away from home. 'Yeah, sure, I'll go with you.' And then when he wrote that note to his mom, 'don't worry, I'll be back in a couple of days.' They were so lucky when that woman in Iowa fed them and they hitch-hiked back home to South Bend."

While Advantage Health is Herr's primary focus, he and Barb have been staunch loyalists for Saint Mary's capital invest-ment and fundraising. They're real champions and advocates for the hospital. They are true angels for our organization. "My wife has been active with Grand Girlfriends. We go to as many hos-pital functions as we can and support them financially. We were involved with the Lacks Cancer Center, the Hausenstein Neuroscience Center and Sophia's House, the new guest house on Saint Mary's downtown campus," said Herr.

John Benz remains one of Herr's greatest cheerleaders. "I don't want to give Bob too much credit otherwise he'll get a big head. But I don't think an ordinary accountant could do what he has done. Bob must have had something that others recognized in South Bend. For him to come up here to Grand Rapids from Indiana and do what he did is pretty amazing!"

And so maybe it all comes down to that character thing, that it takes more than mere talent to keep you on top. "Most talents are to some extent a gift," said composer John Luther. "Good character, by contrast, is not given to us. We have to build it piece by piece by thought, choice, courage and determination."

Frequently, like the song, Bob and Barb Herr will go back to South Bend, back home again to Indiana to where it all began, "to catch a moonbeam on the water, the gleaming candlelight still shining bright through the sycamores, through the fields they used to roam like fancy paints on memory's canvas." They will go to a local football game, drive through the old neighborhoods and share a lot of good stories. It is always a nostalgic journey. Most of the old gang is gone now, but the memories, like deep roots, remain.

Unprofoundly profound – when it comes to Bob Herr, it is just like what Eileen Elias Freeman wrote in her *The Angels' Little Instruction Book*: "Precious and rare, angels are direct creations of God, each one a unique Master's piece."

The Shepherd-in-Chief

Most Reverend Walter A. Hurley
Bishop of Grand Rapids

"You did not choose me, but I chose you and appointed you to go and bear fruit – fruit that will last. Then the Father will give you whatever you ask in my name."

-John 15:16

W hen His Excellency the Most Reverend Walter A. Hurley was officially installed in the late summer of 2005 as the Eleventh Bishop of the Diocese of Grand Rapids, Monsignor Bill Duncan gave him a tour of the city. Stopping in front of the Cathedral of Saint Andrew, Duncan noticed the ornate corner stone on the northeast wall with its timeless inscription that read *"Egglesia St. Andrea, Die Maii 30, A.D. 1875."* Duncan, who had done his homework and knew that Bishop Hurley was born on May 30, said in jest, "Well look, we even had your birthday inscribed on the cathedral!" With an equal yet subtle Irish wit, Bishop Hurley answered with an ear-to-ear grin, "I think that the year is incorrect!"

The age of Walter A. Hurley may very well have begun on a humorous note, but from his first day on the job, he was all business. "I'm going to be here for a long time," he told a crowd of 1,000 at his Mass of Installation. He explained his mission based on tradition. "Let's just build on what we have," Hurley told Mon-

157

signor Duncan. It was Hurley's persistent eye to the future, not the past, on which he would build the Diocese, a mission that had been entrusted to him by Pope Benedict XVI.

Like his priestly predecessors, Bishop Hurley dedicated himself and the Church to a ministry of worship, education, healing and service. It was an outreach that would serve West Michigan's Catholics well, ensuring not only his own success and the growth and achievement of the Diocese but also Saint Mary's Health Care.

On the fourth floor of the contemporary Cathedral Square Center, Bishop Walter Hurley's office is a simple yet modern inner sanctum. With a caring eye, he overlooks the intersection of Wealthy Street and Division Avenue on the edge of Grand Rapids' Heartside neighborhood. Compared to the Bishop's former quarters at the aging St. Joseph Seminary on Burton Street that had served the Diocese for decades, Cathedral Square became a jewel in the crown for West Michigan Catholics. The building was Hurley's vision that evolved during his tenure and became a reality thanks to the generous contributions of donors and diocesan parishes alike. Dedicated in September 2008, stately and majestic, Cathedral Square celebrates the vibrancy of the area's Catholic community.

As the eleventh in a long line of celebrated bishops, Walter A. Hurley, the Prelate of the Diocese, is part of an astonishing legacy of leadership for West Michigan Catholics. Just across the hall from Hurley's Cathedral Square office is a portrait of Henry J. Richter, the very first Bishop of the Diocese. It hangs on the east wall of the fourth floor conference room. Appointed by Pope

Leo XIII in 1883, German-born Richter, described as very learned, modest and of a retiring disposition, served the newly established Diocese until 1916, a span of 33 years. With intricate brush strokes that reveal even the veins and wrinkles in his hands, Richter's portrait is stunning and illustrates the skills of the artist as much as it honors the subject. The placement of his lace vestments and purple garments reflects the stature of the man, right down to the ornate Bible in his grasp and the weighty Celtic cross that hangs from Richter's neck. It sets a tone, a style and a power of legacy only steps away from Hurley's office. Above all, the portrait strikes a stately and symbolic pose emblematic of contemporary Catholic tradition in the Diocese that has been handed down across the decades, to the Eleventh Bishop, Walter A. Hurley.

"We are always reminded by Saint Paul that 'there are many gifts of the same spirit,'" said Monsignor Duncan pondering the ten bishops that have preceded Walter Hurley (Richter, Gallagher, Kelly, Pinten, Plagens, Haas, Babcock, Breitenbeck, Rose, Britt). "Each came very human to the office relying on God's grace to guide them. Each one brought a different style of management, spirituality and communications skills, to the job, but always focusing on the same mission, service to the church and carrying out the mission that had been entrusted to them."

Shortly after Bishop Hurley arrived in Grand Rapids, Monsignor Duncan, who also serves the Diocese as its Vicar General, took the new Bishop out to Resurrection Cemetery. There in the in the late afternoon stillness, "where the air was full of farewells to the dead," Longfellow wrote, the two men stood by that section of the cemetery where most of the Diocese's previous bishops had been laid to rest. Solemn and somber, Monsignor Duncan looked down and pointed out the brass name plates that had been planted into the hallowed ground at the graves of the other bishops, and said that "this is where you are going to go." Bishop Hurley, who rarely missed an opportunity for a humorous rejoinder, said, "I just arrived and you've already got me buried!" It was yet another example of Hurley's quick wit and self-deprecating humor.

I first met Bishop Hurley when he arrived in Grand Rapids in 2005. I had been President and CEO at Saint Mary's Health Care for five years. After Bishop Kevin Britt died unexpectedly in 2004, there was concern at Saint Mary's that the next bishop would not be as engaged as Britt. But with Bishop Hurley, Saint Mary's was not disappointed. Not only did he have a grand vision for the Diocese, but he had a grand vision for the hospital as well.

Saint Mary's was an ideal fit for Hurley; he looked across the Diocese with an analytical eye. He saw the Cathedral of Saint Andrew as the heart of Catholic worship and saw Catholic Central High School, and all the parish schools across the Diocese, including Aquinas College, as the hub of Catholic education. He also saw the collective Diocese as a vehicle for service to the community, and he saw Saint Mary's Health Care as an outreach for the healing ministry of the Church. Like spokes on a wheel, each core discipline was perfectly suited to Hurley's grand vision.

Walter Hurley grew up in the provincial capital of Fredericton in New Brunswick, Canada. As a young parochial school student in Saint Dunstan's Parish, Hurley recalls wanting to be a priest from his earliest years. "It was always something I was looking to and wanted to do," he said.

Fredericton, a small city nestled along the banks of the St. John River, is described as a warm and friendly place with the diverse tastes of a cosmopolitan city. Hurley grew up on a tree-lined street replete with Victorian homes and a quaint neighborhood sensibility. The community was known then, as it is today, for its vibrant cultural life and university influence.

The earliest history of St. Dunstan's, the church Hurley attended in Fredericton, can be traced back to 1611 when Jesuit missionaries worked in the area and ministered to the converted Indians. For many years there was no church in the town so Catholic families traveled to French Village 11 miles away for Sunday Mass. Eventually, a parish was established and a church was built. The town selected St. Dunstan as its patron saint. Later, the parish attracted impoverished European immigrants who had escaped the Irish potato famine of 1848. A series of disastrous fires destroyed over twenty buildings in Fredericton but the Catholic Cathedral and the bishop's residence survived thanks to St. Dunstan's attentive parishioners who, it is said, covered the roof with themselves to protect the church from the flames.

Born in 1937, Walter Hurley lived a typical Canadian middle class life on Victoria Street. Like many young Catholic boys, he was influenced by a strong role model, the Right Rev. Dr. Charles Boyd, who led St. Dunstan. "I had a great deal of respect and admiration for him," said Hurley. "I was sort of inspired by him. He was a community leader. He was a very bright man, very intelligent. I just admired him."

Monsignor Duncan said that is often the case. "Priests are adult role models that we look to. You have that internal calling of God, but it is confirmed by seeing that modeled, in the priestly life of others. And it attracts you and you say, 'I think I can live that.'"

When he was 17, Hurley's family moved to Detroit. "My father needed a job. He had sisters and brothers already living in Detroit. It was kind of a natural evolution," Hurley said.

Before entering the seminary, Hurley worked for the Royal Bank of Canada in Windsor and Manufacturers National Bank in Detroit, and finally for a manufacturing company. Eventually, with his seminary degree in hand, he became a U.S. citizen in 1961.

Walter Hurley's priestly odyssey was unpredictable. At the suggestion of Cardinal Szoka, the Archbishop of Detroit, he earned a degree in canon law from Catholic University and later became Szoka's Judicial Vicar and Chief of Staff. After an assignment in Rome with the Vatican administration and having served various parishes, he became pastor of Our Lady of Sorrows community in Farmington where he stayed for 13 years before his appointment as Auxiliary Bishop in Detroit. And then came the call from the Apostolic Nuncio in Washington, D.C. – that the Holy Father had appointed him Bishop of the Diocese of Grand Rapids in 2005 to succeed Bishop Kevin Britt.

Hurley often jokes that his next move would be to the nursing home. "He had chosen a retirement place," said Mary Haarman, former director of communications for the Diocese. "That's what he was going to do." But God had other plans for 68-year-old Hurley.

"When Bishop Hurley came and celebrated Chrism Mass with us before his appointment, it was at a time when we were without a bishop here," said Haarman.

"I didn't come to look the divine part nor to be looked over. I just came to celebrate Chrism Mass," Hurley told his audience prior to his calling. But then it became official; he would come to Grand Rapids.

"When we made the announcement to the media," said Haarman, "we had a big chest we brought out, and we said, 'now this shows that you're really going to stay.' It was just a big old trunk instead of an overnight bag!"

Even though he had spent much of his time on the east side of the state, Grand Rapids was Hurley's kind of town. "We always would tease him," said Monsignor Duncan. "Many of our bishops, with the exception of Bishop Rose, have historically come from Detroit."

Hurley quickly grew to love Grand Rapids and West Michigan. "He sees the Church as part of 'community,'" said Haarman. "He loves our community. He believes there is such a faith element here and such a strong sense of stewardship, people getting in there and doing. A lot of people don't realize that this is a Catholic community and the largest religious denomination in the area."

Bishop Hurley appreciates Grand Rapids' faith-based culture. "I really like that. It's most unusual for so many leaders in the community to be church people, belonging to one or the other churches. They're connected," said Hurley. "And for the most part, they worship on a regular basis. This is a wonderful place to be! It's a vibrant place. Grand Rapids is a small 'big town.' It has a lot of the advantages of a large city. We're almost like a mini-Chicago."

In short order, Bishop Hurley became tied to Saint Mary's. He and I became fast friends. Soon he established an agenda for the hospital and the Diocese that fit his master plan. His vision and mine were quite compatible. He was always very supportive even when we had some difficult issues to work through at the hospital. Once, Bishop Hurley even attended a board meeting. That was quite unprecedented! The board loved it!

"I remember the Bishop coming to our meeting. It was memorable and significant," said board member, Russ Visner. "His visit reinforced how important Saint Mary's Health Care's mission is to the community."

Former board chair, Nancy Kennedy, recalls the meeting too. "It just made sense that he would come since Saint Mary's operates at his pleasure as a Catholic institution. That he came to be with us was really secondary to what the Bishop stands for. It should happen more. When hospital patients look out their window and see the Cathedral, there is such a focus on the cross that points toward Heaven."

Monsignor Duncan, who used to work at Saint Mary's, believes Hurley was the perfect fit. "Bishop Hurley is very much tied to the hospital. There you see the Catholic Church in all of its expressions. That is where the Church's healing mission is carried out. So all of this is in one local focus right in the heart of the city. You see the Church doing what it is called to do by Christ – to gather for worship, to educate, to heal and to serve. And the hospital provides that healing component."

Hurley concurs. "Our working relationship has been very good. When we were in the process of developing the Cathedral Square project, Saint Mary's people were extraordinarily supportive. When we took down the old Saint Andrew's School building, our two campuses became connected. I've seen a lot of development at Saint Mary's. The Hauenstein Neuroscience Center came to be just about the time I arrived in Grand Rapids, the new emergency room, too. So the hospital is very much connected to the Catholic community and very much a part of it."

Growing up in New Brunswick, Bishop Hurley had Irish roots that are wide and deep. "I am of Irish decent," he said. "I really never wanted to know too much about my family tree, my ancestors, for fear of what I might find!" he said laughingly. "I'm more interested in moving ahead than I am in looking back."

Part of his moving ahead philosophy included the development and planning of Cathedral Square. The previous location for the Diocese at St. Joseph's Seminary on Burton Street, in Bishop Hurley's eyes, was no longer working. "As a Catholic community out there, we were all scattered throughout the city," said Mary Haarman. "So by bringing everyone together, it is more effective as a working environment, for collaboration. I think the key thing is that all the administrative offices are right at Cathedral Square. And this allows everyone to be much more effective and supportive of the schools and the parishes."

Monsignor Duncan admires Bishop Hurley's respect for tradition but also his fluidity, his energy to keep moving forward. "He's always been one to set the horizon, to keep the motion moving ahead, not nostalgia for the sake of nostalgia, not just to say 'let's stay here because this is where we are comfortable,'" said Duncan. "It's all about moving us out of our comfort zone. How do we become more vibrant? How do we share the Good News?"

Haarman, who has worked for four bishops, including Hurley, is impressed with his broad vision and his ability to analyze where the Diocese is and where it needs to go. "That has guided him through this whole piece," she said. "He's very big on technology. The Diocese is right where it needs to be. It is expanding its website, we are tweeting, we are on Facebook. And the Bishop is a bit of a news junkie. He's up on what's happening in the world and in the Church."

Duncan does not disagree. "We were way behind the eight ball with technology, and he comes in and says 'let's get this going, let's get wired, let's do what we need to do.'"

Bishop Hurley is very direct. If you ask him a question, you're going to get an answer. "It may not always be the answer you want to hear," said Haarman. "But that's what I like about him. You always know his position, where he stands and why. It's just very obvious."

Duncan admires Hurley's transparency. "That is really a blessing in today's Church. You might not always agree with him, but you know where you stand. He doesn't play games. He just says 'here's the way to deal with this, let's go.'"

Bishop Hurley's days are full and varied. "I normally visit parishes on the weekends," he said. "We have over one hundred parishes across 11 counties, and I've visited each one at least three times. So there's that dimension."

Shepherd-in-Chief is an apt description of Walter Hurley. The Diocese is a huge organization, including Saint Mary's Health Care, Aquinas College, and Catholic Charities. "I enjoy it. It's a big job" said Hurley.

"His day varies," said Duncan. "He might begin by celebrating Mass in the morning. He devotes time to prayer, and then he's either meeting with the Diocesan staff or the clergy or other organizations, other community organizations. The Bishop is the shepherd of the whole flock of the Diocese. Shepherd is always such a great image. From a business term, yes, he is like a CEO. But from a much more pastoral perspective, Bishop Hurley has been entrusted with this care-giving position with the Roman Catholic Church."

Haarman admires Hurley's ease of access. "He has an open door policy, which is very helpful," she said. "Clergy and staff can just go in and talk to him. They don't have to have an appointment. If his door is open, he'll see you, and that, I think, is phenomenal!"

Combined with Hurley's ease of access is the Bishop's illustrious sense of humor. "He's not a joke-teller," said Duncan. "He's just a subtle, witty person, always quite self-deprecating."

In the summer of 2011, Hurley had heart surgery. "I'd go with him to the hospital," said Duncan. "We'd see these slides and images of his heart, the heart valves and everything and he'd say, 'Oh, Monsignor, now you can tell the other priests that the Bishop does have a heart, and I have seen the proof.'"

"And thanks to good care and skilled doctors, his surgery went very well. 'For those whose prayers were answered, I am grateful,' he said, and 'for those prayers that were not answered, better luck next time!' And that always got a laugh! He's a good, good man," said Duncan. "He's a good leader."

"Admiring the portrait of the Diocese's very first Bishop, Henry J. Richter, that hangs in the fourth floor conference room at Cathedral Square, I am overcome by the power of tradition. It never fails to impress and move me," said Duncan.

"There's a thread that goes through all the bishops of the Diocese," said Duncan. "How do we keep the faith, how do we remain faithful to the Gospel and live it out as a Catholic community until the Lord returns? How many more bishops will there be until Christ returns? We don't know. But each one will be here for a time in history, a mortal time."

Finally, Bishop Hurley is very much tuned in to the religious concept of being "chosen." When he speaks to young people he always impresses on them the notion of being chosen.

"He's so relaxed with young people," said Mary Haarman.

Speaking to a group of students at the Cathedral of Saint Andrew who had gathered for a Confirmation ceremony, Hurley stood before them dressed in his colorful red vestments and wearing his ceremonial miter. He looked down on the 113 students who had come that night to be confirmed.

"You have been chosen, not by some human person, but you have been chosen by God," Hurley said. "Tonight we celebrate another choice that God has made of you. He is asking you to work in the 'family business.' Now the family business is pretty simple. It's proclaiming the Good News —a message of hope, a message of God's love. And so that's the real choice that God has made of us, to share in His saving work. So tonight we give thanks to the Lord for having chosen you. You are now among his chosen people. You have been set aside to be bearers of good news in the world in which we live, to bring the message of God's love and His message of hope to a troubled and difficult world."

Indeed, "You did not choose me, but I chose you and appointed you to go and bear fruit – fruit that will last. Then the Father will give you whatever you ask in my name."

Epilogue

Since the spring of 2000 I have driven from my home in Cascade to my office at Saint Mary's in downtown Grand Rapids. Over the years my drive to work has become a sense of ritual; for me it was almost like a form of celebration, a daily rite. I will miss that traditional drive into town.

I have written before that each day when I arrived at my office, I would begin the day by studying the cross atop the Cathedral of Saint Andrew, clearly visible from my office window. Like a barometer, the cross became my friend, my personal predictor of how the day would go. It was transformational and reassuring. Regardless of the season, when the sun struggled to rise just right in the eastern sky over Grand Rapids, the cross, lit by a beam of light, glowed the most magnificent color of gold. Catching the sun's rays like a great shining star, the cross let me know it was going to be a good day. These were always the best of mornings. They filled me with a solemn pride. The cross served as a reminder of God's presence and how softly Jesus walks in our lives. And each day, it renewed my commitment to Saint Mary's, to our mission, to our patients, to our magnificent staff of healers, and to God. What a wondrous way to begin each day!

When I left Spectrum Health in 1999, a friend gave me a CD performed by her favorite singer, Twila Paris. One of the songs on the CD, "God is in Control," was particularly meaningful. It helped keep me focused during my job search. It gave me great comfort during that time when I didn't know where I would go or land or be. As she sings her song, Twila Paris cautions that this isn't the time for fears, rather it is a time to rely on what is in your heart. It is not a time to lose focus or get carried away by emotions. There has always been one thing that has been true and holds the world together and that is the control that God provides. If we recognize this, we will never be shaken.

You may have heard the saying, "Find a job you love and you will never work a day in your life." I have loved serving Saint Mary's. Every day has been a blessing, a voyage of discovery, a time of undivided tenderness, and an opportunity to serve God. I truly believe that I was meant to be at Saint Mary's Health Care. God was and is in control. He has a plan for each of us, a ministry He is calling us to do. We only need to remember during those moments of doubt that we are not alone in our journey, that God is in control. As Bishop Kevin Britt believed, "God opens a door and we walk through it." Or as Bishop Walter Hurley instructs, "we are chosen by God to do His work, to become part of His family."

In times of great stress or fear or doubt, I pray for wisdom; when trouble looms, I often turn to the Bible. I find Matthew 6:25-34 a source of comfort.

> *Therefore I tell you, do not be anxious about your life, what you shall eat or what you shall drink, nor about your body, what you shall put on. Is not life more than food, and the body more than clothing?*

Look at the birds of the air: they neither sow nor reap nor gather into barns, and yet your heavenly Father feeds them. Are you not of more value than they?

And which of you by being anxious can add one cubit to his span of life?

And why are you anxious about clothing? Consider the lilies of the field, how they grow; they neither toil nor spin; yet I tell you, even Solomon in all his glory was not arrayed like one of these.

But if God so clothes the grass of the field, which today is alive and tomorrow is thrown into the oven, will he not much more clothe you, O men of little faith?

Therefore do not be anxious, saying, 'What shall we eat?' or 'What shall we drink?' or 'What shall we wear?'

For the Gentiles seek all these things; and your heavenly Father knows that you need them all.

But seek first his kingdom and his righteousness, and all these things shall be yours as well.

Therefore do not be anxious about tomorrow, for tomorrow will be anxious for itself. Let the day's own trouble be sufficient for the day.

Throughout this book I have tried to express my sense of appreciation for my years at Saint Mary's. Earlier I quoted Cicero – "that there is no quality I would rather have and be thought to have than gratitude, for it is not only the greatest virtue but the mother of all the rest." And so I am deeply grateful to all of you who have lifted me up on the wings of angels in this healing ministry of Jesus Christ, and to all of you who have been part of God's plan for me at Saint Mary's Health Care. And so I leave you with the simplest form of gratitude—a thankful heart.

The men and women profiled in this book are all angels among us. Where would Saint Mary's be without them, or I without all of you? Thanking them and thanking you, my beloved friends everywhere within earshot, somehow seems insufficient. The lyrics from the song *Angels Among Us* by the American country music band Alabama keep playing back in my mind. The lyrics remind us that angels come to us in our darkest hours and often show up in the most unlikely places. They guide us and bless us with their kindness.

And so I leave you with a thankful heart. Let it be my form of thanksgiving to all of the angels in my life, my grateful prayer. You are everywhere and everything to me. What more can I say but thank you. Thank you. Thanks be to God.

Epilogue

References

Acknowledgments

William Shakespeare, *King Henry VI, Part II, Act I, scene i.*

Claudia Gould is the Director of the Institute of Contemporary Art at the University of Pennsylvania in Philadelphia.

Preface

Cicero (106 – 43 B.C.), was a Roman philosopher and statesman.

A Messenger From God

Eileen Elias Freeman. *The Angels' Little Instruction Book.* New York: Grand Central Publishing, 1994.

Laurie Beth Jones. *Jesus CEO: Using Ancient Wisdom for Visionary Leadership.* New York: Hyperion, 1992.

The Wind Behind My Back

Dwight D. Eisenhower (1890-1969), was the 34th President of the United States.

Joseph Campbell (1904-1987), was an American mythologist, writer and lecturer.

Pindar (552-443 B.C.), was an ancient Greek poet.

Henry Wadsworth Longfellow (1807-1882), was an American poet and educator.

Rod McKuen. "Age is better." *A Safe Place to Land.* Indianola, Iowa: Cheval Publishing, 2001.

An Angel Gets His Wings

Peter M. Wege (1920 -), is one of Grand Rapids' premier philanthropists and best known for his environmental activism.

Frank Capra, Director. *It's a Wonderful Life*, (1946).

George F. Burba (1887-1965), was a newspaper editorial writer.

Henry David Thoreau (1817-1862), was an American author, poet, essayist and philosopher.

Desiree Joseph Mercier (1851-1926), was a Belgian cardinal.

Booker T. Washington (1856-1915), was an African American educator.

An Inspired Journey

Mahatma Gandhi (1869-1948), was a political and ideological leader in India.

John Dryden, *The Imitation of Horace, book iii, Ode 29, line 65.*

A Righteous Man

Michael LeBoeuf (1942 -), is an American business author and former management professor at the University of New Orleans.

Michael Porter (1947-), is the professor and director of the Institute for Strategy and Competitiveness at the Harvard Business School.

Robert Louis Stevenson (1850-1894), was a Scottish novelist, poet and essayist.

Fred R. Shapiro (1954-), is editor of *The Yale Book of Quotations*.

Lou Holtz (1937-), is a retired football coach, motivational speaker and ESPN personality.

Alfred Tennyson, "The Vision of Sin." (1809-1892).

Frank Muir (1920-1998), was a British actor, comedian and BBC radio personality.

W.E.P. French. www.thecorkscrewdiary.tv/

Robert Mallet (1810-1881), was an Irish scientist.

Washington Irving (1783-1859), was an American author, essayist and biographer.

The Altar Boy

John C. Canepa (1930 -), is formerly Old Kent Bank's Chairman and CEO and Consulting Principle for Crowe Chizek in Grand Rapids, Michigan.

Jonathan Alter (1957-), is a journalist and author.

The People's Bishop

Dorothy Day (1897-1980), was an American journalist, social activist and devout Catholic convert.

The Man For All Seasons

Joe Girard (1928 -), is an author and motivational speaker.

Robert D. Putnam. *Bowling Alone: The Collapse and Revival of American Community.* New York: Simon & Schuster, 2000.

Tom Wolfe. *The Bonfire of the Vanities:* A Novel. New York: Farrar, Strauss and Giroux, 1987.

Yogi Berra (1925-), former major league baseball player and manager.

The Kid From Pewamo

Theodore Hesburgh (1917 -   ), is President Emeritus of the University of Notre Dame.

John Cougar Mellencamp, "Small Town," *Scarecrow,* 1985.

www.lyonstownship.ioniacounty.org/history.htm

Abigail Van Buren (1918-2013), was an American advice columnist.

Washington Irving (1783-1859), was an American author, essayist and biographer.

Edgar Lee Masters. "The Hill." *Spoon River Anthology,* 1916.

Mark Twain (1835-1910), was an American author.

Working Together Toward Holiness

Luciano de Crescenzo (1928 -   ), is an Italian actor, director and writer.

Unprofoundly Profound

Proverbs, 3:3 New Revised Standard Version

John Wooden (1910-2010), was an American basketball coach.

Eric Honeycutt is a professional photographer and writer. www.care2.com/ecards/bio/1013

Abraham Lincoln (1809-1865), was the 16th President of the United States.

James Russell Lowell (1819-1891), was an American poet, critic and diplomat.

H. Jackson Brown, Jr. *Life's Little Instruction Book: 511 Suggestions, Observations and Reminders on how to live a happy and rewarding life.* Nashville: Thomas Nelson, 2000.

Thomas Paine (1737-1809), was an American author and pamphleteer. David Foster Wallace. *The Pale King.* New York: Back Bay Books, 2011.

William Shakespeare. *Romeo and Juliet, Act II, Scene iii, line 94.*

Pietro Aretino (1492-1556), was an Italian author, playwright, poet and satirist.

Mark Twain. *The Adventures of Tom Sawyer.* Philadelphia: American Publishing Company, 1876.

John Luther (1953-), is an American musician and composer.

Ballard MacDonald and James F. Hanley, "Back Home Again In Indiana," 1917.

Eileen Elias Freeman. *The Angels' Little Instruction Book.* New York: Grand Central Publishing, 1994.

Shepherd-in-Chief

John, 15: 16 New International Version

Henry Wadsworth Longfellow (1807-1882), was an American poet and educator.

Epilogue

Twila Paris, *Beyond a Dream,* "God is in Control," Star Song, 1993. CD.

Matthew, 6:25-34 Revised Standard Version

Don Goodman and Becky Hobbs. "Angels Among Us" 1993

The Author

PHIL McCORKLE has been President and CEO of Saint Mary's Health Care since April of 2000. Under his direction the hospital has grown significantly. Since 2002 Saint Mary's has built and opened the Richard J. Lacks, Sr. Cancer Center; the Hauenstein Neuroscience Center, a comprehensive neuroscience facility; Saint Mary's Southwest, an expansive ambulatory care facility; and Sophia's House, the hospital's downtown Grand Rapids guest house. Previous to his Saint Mary's appointment, McCorkle served as an executive at Butterworth Hospital, DeVos Children's Hospital and Spectrum Health in Grand Rapids. He is married to Gayle McCorkle. They have two sons and two grandsons.

MIKE GRASS is a freelance writer who lives and works in Grand Rapids. His work includes the Emmy Award-nominated PBS documentary, *Time and Chance—Gerald Ford's Appointment With History* and the PBS film, *America's Senator—The Unexpected Odyssey of Arthur Vandenberg.*